Original 5

Navigating a Blended Family

Georgie Moody

with the Moody/Bain Crew

Limits of Liability and Disclaimer of Warranty
The author and publisher shall not be liable for your misuse of this material. The purpose of this book is to educate and entertain. The author and/or publisher do not guarantee that anyone following these techniques, suggestions, tips, ideas, or strategies will become successful. The author and/or publisher shall have neither liability nor responsibility to anyone with respect to any loss or damage caused, or alleged to be caused, directly or indirectly by the information contained in this book. If expert assistance is required, the services of a competent professional should be sought.

Copy Editor: Donna Moody
Developmental Editors: Pamela Bain, Wayne Moody
Creative Direction: "Original 5"
Author Photo: JMC Photography
Cover Design: MS Design & Photography
Interior Format Design: Laura Brown
Interior Artwork Drawings: The "Littles" of the Moody/Bain Crew

ISBN: 978-1-941749-71-5
4-P Publishing
Chattanooga, TN 37411
LCCN: 2017911064
Printed in the United States of America

"Original 5" - Blended Resources

We want to hear about you!
Connect with other blended families like yours by joining the "Original 5" blended family.
Get the stories, tips, new releases, and downloads.

Like and follow our page at:
www.facebook.com/navigatingablendedfamily

Dedication

This book is dedicated to the "Original 5" (Belinda, Teresa, Jayne, Michael, and Jessica), who *navigated* their way straight into my heart.

Acknowledgements

"Original 5": For your creative direction and openness in sharing your stories.

Belinda: You are a wonderful wife and mother. Your aspirations illicit fervent hope even when life looks bleak because you are a visionary. You just add sparkles! I love you Belinda!

Teresa: You live with ferocity and are persistent in pursuing your dreams even when life takes you on a different path. Your passion is intoxicating! I love you Teresa!

Jayne: You are a fabulous wife and mother. Your humor lifts me up when I need it the most and your tenacity is contagious. Your creativity inspires me! I love you Jayne!

Michael: You are a marvelous (remarkable and particularly excellent – Ha! Just like your chapter title) husband and father. You process life thoughtfully but keep people guessing in a way that is mystifying. You continually amaze me! I love you Michael!

Jessica: You live with intention and nothing much ruffles your feathers. Your composure is soothing when chaos erupts. Your quiescent cleverness astounds me! I love you Jessica!

<u>Wayne</u>: My husband and father of the "Original 5" and Developmental Editor. For your input, your motivation and for championing my new adventure. Falling in love with and marrying you has led to more than I ever imagined. Just look at this family! I love you Moody Man!

<u>Pam</u>: Mother of the "Original 5" and Developmental Editor. For your perception, your creativity and your willingness to jump in head first with me on our many ventures. Ready for more? I sure hope so, because I treasure our friendship and this family!

<u>John</u>: Stepfather of the "Original 5". For your thoughtfulness, receptiveness and for connecting with all of us in a way I always hoped for. I couldn't think of a better guy to stepparent the "Original 5" with!

<u>Wes</u>: Half brother of the "Original 5". For being helpful, inventive, and understanding of the time I spent on this project. Thank you for your artistic drawing in this book. I love your creativity and how you love this family!

<u>Alan, Christopher Alan & Brooke</u>: The spouses of Belinda, Jayne and Michael. For your own experiences coming from blended families and marrying into and being such an important part of all of us. Also, for allowing me extra time with your spouses and supporting them as they helped me with this book. By the way, you guys are next! Sequel???

Brian: Boyfriend of Teresa. For being a part of us and supporting Teresa as she helped me with this book. Looking forward to us all riding in your boat and listening to you play your ukulele in the moonlight!

Venessa, Alaina, Daniel, Brenden, Cassidy, Audrey & Chloe: Grandkids. I love being "Gigi" to you (thanks to Venessa naming me as such when she was two years old). Thank you for your wonderful drawings in this book and being a part of our beautiful family. I love you so much!

Corey, Marisa & Robby: Stepsiblings of the "Original 5". I am so happy you three are a part of our family. Your stepmom, Pam, is the glue that binds us together even though we don't have traditional family connections. Looking forward to more fun together. I love you!

My family, Wayne's family, Pam's family, John's family: Our extended families outside of the 23 of us. Thank you for raising us with the experiences and values that have allowed us to be the people we are today and the family we have become together. We love you all!

Sylvia Banks: Mentor. Over a year ago, when you asked me to review your book, "The 7 Pillars of a Noble Woman", we agreed you would be a part of the book I would write as well. The journey we took together became more than what I thought it would be. Thank you for encouraging me, for going above and beyond as my mentor and for your friendship. I look forward to more collaboration in the future!

Anthony Bledsoe: Family friend 23+ years. You have seen this family beginning, middle and end. You bless us all in so many ways. Thank you for introducing our story. We love you and your family!

Laura Brown: Coach. Thank you for finding and following your purpose in the creation of S.W.A.T. Book Camp (www.swatbookcamp.com). You are an inspiration in overcoming challenges and pursuing dreams. I fully understand the slogan you use – "This is **not** your momma's writing group!"

Teresa Cantrell, John Di Candilo: Beta Readers. The concept of a beta reader was new to me, but both of you stepped up and gave me more than I expected. Thank you for your friendship and your valuable input on the words we trust will encourage other families like ours!

<u>Donna Moody</u>: Copy Editor and my sister-in-law. The true definition of Grammar Nazi/Nerd. My favorite part in this endeavor with you was your story about realizing I can write a little better than I speak (inside joke)! Thank you for your editing insight and for your friendship!

<u>Michael Simmons</u>: MS Design and Photography. Thank you for your visual expression of this story from the view of the "Original 5". You captured the book cover perfectly!

About the Author

Georgie is a ghostwriter. Her passion is to inspire people to pursue their potential and cultivate their unique design. She achieves this by encouraging them to impact others through written words.

She was educated at Tennessee Technological University and is a certified Public Housing Manager with NAHRO. She has worked in the subsidized housing industry for 16+ years.

Writing, reading, painting, anything creative and project management are all things Georgie enjoys. She and Pam, the mom of the "Original 5", create together in the planning of family events and gifts.

Georgie and Wayne have been married for almost 13 years and live in North Georgia outside of Chattanooga, TN. They have a blended family of six children, two sons-in law, one daughter-in law, seven grandchildren, one mom of "Original 5" children, her husband and his three children - a total of 23.

Contents

Foreword

Anthony Bledsoe has been a friend of the family for 23 years and is a minister and city employee in Pulaski, TN. He and his wife, Mattie, have two adult children, Chris and Markeyta. Anthony has witnessed all phases of togetherness, separation and restoration of the Moody/Bain family. He shares his thoughts below:

We live in an imperfect world where sometimes things become disjointed. Homes, relationships, families and friends are what we both treasure and love, yet they can be easily shattered. We live and cope with these areas of division every day.

In this book, you will discover how God's grace along with our willingness to find His healing can mend even the deepest areas of destruction.

Over the years, my wife, Mattie, and I have had the privilege of serving many of the families in our community. We have seen firsthand how God can masterfully blend two broken families into one God honoring, God loving family. The Moody and

Bain crew are living proof that no matter where your family is right now, there is hope for brighter and better days.

Relationships can be healed and joy can be restored. Once again, life can have real meaning. Members of this beautiful family make it clear in these pages that you don't have to have all the answers, just a willingness to get started and keep moving forward.

Anthony Bledsoe

1

Genesis of a Blended Family

*"Blended families reflect second
chances and the belief
that love conquers all."*
-Georgie Moody

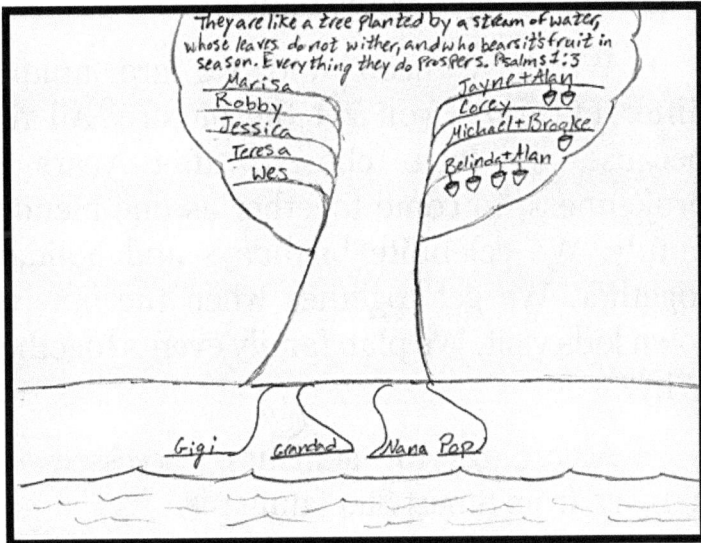

"Blended Family Tree" by Venessa

"Original 5"

From 1 Family to 2

Five kids, play excitedly together, not knowing their world was about to fall apart...

I am the stepmom of these five kids, who ranged from ages seven to seventeen when I first started dating their father (who I married thirteen months later). We are the Moody/Bain blended family.

We have three other family names, due to marriages. To avoid confusion, we refer to ourselves as the Moody/Bain crew.

We have been told we are unique, different, crazy...you get the picture. All this because we have chosen, after years of brokenness, to come together as one blended family. We celebrate birthdays and holidays together. We get together when the out- of-town kids visit. We plan family events together. Why?

According to statistics, accessed on 3/15/17, from Smart Stepfamilies™.

www.smartstepfamilies.com/view/statistics

- ❖ "One-third of all students in the US will have a stepparent at age 18..."
- ❖ "...40% of families are blended families..."
- ❖ "On average, it takes more time for a child to adjust to a parent's remarriage than to the original parental divorce."

Please check out more from this great resource. They have free articles, books authored by Ron L. Deal and information on conferences.

Broken Family

We all want less stress in our lives, a feeling of peace, especially when we are in a blended family situation. Life is difficult enough without the added challenges of trying to reduce tension between households, helping kids who are on edge because they don't know how to balance time between parents, and kids dealing with stepparents who were not a part of this whole thing, to begin with.

So, how do you go from a broken family to a blended family?

Blended families are dealing with loss. Loss of togetherness, loss of family routine, loss of their previous stability. A guide doesn't just fall out of the sky with all the new rules and directions on how to go from point A to Z. This is a journey and not an easy or short one.

How do you get to Z? How do you just go from A to B? We don't have all the answers. We were not perfect at this ourselves, and we are still not finished with our journey. What we <u>can</u> give you is hope. Hope that you can come together, that you can forgive and heal from all the hurts. Hope that you can be in the same room enjoying yourself as a new kind of family – a crazy, inclusive blended family.

How Did We Do It?

Again, we don't have a guide on this whole blended family thing. We can tell you how we started, how we overcame challenges and how we continue still to choose and work at being together.

One way to start is with something we all require to live: Food.

According to Mirele Mann's article, "9 Scientifically Proven Reasons to Eat Dinner as a Family" accessed on 3/15/17 at www.goodnet.org/articles/9-scientifically-proven-reasons-to-eat-dinner-as-family "Families who eat together, stay together."

Three of her nine reasons to eat together include:

* ❖ "Family dinners mean better family relationships"
* ❖ "Family dinners lead to greater happiness"
* ❖ "Family dinners relieve stress"

One of the things we started with was a simple family favorite meal in a public space, but more on that later.

Reference

Reference is needed due to the fact there are 23 members of this crazy group. The next two pages are a depiction of how the members align with each other.

Moody/Bain Crew (23 members)

	Wayne married to Georgie	"Original 5"	*Pam* married to John	
half brother of Original 5	Wes	Belinda married to Alan (Venessa, Alaina, Daniel & Brenden)	Corey	stepsiblings of Original 5
		Teresa	Marisa	
		Jayne married to Christopher Alan (Cassidy & Chloe)	Robby	
		Michael married to Brooke (Audrey)		
		Jessica		

The "Littles" (chart in age order)

The "Littles" of our blended family include the nieces, nephews, half brother and younger stepsiblings of the "Original 5". The "Littles", as of this publication, range from ages nine months to 14 years old.

Name	Relationship to Original 5
Venessa	niece
Marisa	stepsister
Alaina	niece
Wes	half brother
Daniel	nephew
Robby	stepbrother
Brenden	nephew
Cassidy	niece
Audrey	niece
Chloe	niece

What to Expect

In each chapter, you will see artwork from the "Littles" of our blended family.

Each "Original 5" as well as their biological parents, will have their own chapter with an introduction, their story, my narration and reflection points.

At the end of each chapter, you will find a "Blender":

- **Activities:** Fun, a word that describes activities we engage in as a blended family. Pam and I (with help from the family) plan and execute these to establish lasting memories. You can use these for your blended family.
- **Recipes:** All families have recipes. Here are some of the Moody/Bain family recipes we use in our homes and when we spend time together.

We have found these two things work well in our group if we leave room for downtime as well.

Remember, you are dealing with different personalities, some new, some old. Not everyone will want to participate in everything. The important thing is to be together, start small and keep going.

Pre-Blended Family Reflections

- Choose to come together.

- Eat together.

- Plan family events together.

Pre- Blended Family Blender

Activity

Camping

Camping was a family favorite when there was just one household. As a blended family group, though, we have not tackled this together just yet. You will almost always find a tent in the yard at most of our family get togethers. We have at least one of the "Original 5", who I think could live outside (wink, wink – Teresa!).

Recipe (from www.justapinch.com)

Polish Kielbasa and Cabbage Soup

(a.k.a. Boiled Dinner/Irish Stew/Cabbage Stew)

Whatever the name of this yummy soup, it is a hit with this group and a tradition pre-blended family! The recipe is easy and quick to make, not to mention economical too. Check out the variations some of the family members have made to the recipe as they have put their spin on it.

Camping

Supplies

- ☐ Camping gear
- ☐ Camping supplies
- ☐ Camping food
- ☐ Tent, camper, cabin, hammock and/or Yurt
- ☐ Sleeping bags, blankets
- ☐ A place to camp!

Directions

- ☐ Spend time together before, during and after planning, setting up and taking down camp. (Be sure to think about how to deal with creatures great and small in your camp area.)
- ☐ Explore your surroundings on a nature hike.
- ☐ Play games together.
- ☐ Cook some yummy camp food over a fire.
- ☐ Tell stories and sleep under the stars.

Polish Kielbasa & Cabbage Soup

Ingredients

- ☐ 1 lb. polish kielbasa, sliced into ¼ inch rounds
- ☐ 2 cups onions, sliced thinly
- ☐ 4 cups green cabbage, shredded
- ☐ 1 Tablespoon fresh garlic, minced
- ☐ 6 cups vegetable stock
- ☐ 2 cups potatoes, peeled and diced
- ☐ 1 teaspoon salt
- ☐ ½ teaspoon pepper

Directions

- ☐ Sauté kielbasa in a large soup pot over medium heat for 5 minutes. Remove kielbasa & set aside.
- ☐ Add onions and cabbage and sauté for 10 minutes, stirring occasionally.
- ☐ Add garlic and sauté for 2 minutes, stirring constantly.

- ☐ Add vegetable stock, potatoes, salt and pepper and sautéed kielbasa.
- ☐ Bring to a boil and simmer for 20 minutes.

Pam's variation (Boiled Dinner)

- ☐ No onion or garlic. Water instead of vegetable stock.
- ☐ Boil potatoes with carrots until easily pierced with a fork.
- ☐ Add kielbasa and then cabbage
- ☐ Heat through – just until cabbage begins to wilt.
- ☐ Season with salt and pepper to taste.

Belinda's variation (Irish Stew):

- ☐ Use smoked beef sausage instead of kielbasa
- ☐ Use potato varieties (4 Yukon, 6 small reds, etc.) and carrot varieties (regular carrots, baby carrots, etc.)
- ☐ Make a purple version using purple potatoes and purple cabbage. (The water turns purple!)

Teresa's variation (Cabbage stew):

- ☐ Brown kielbasa with onions before boiling with potatoes.
- ☐ Use chicken broth instead of water or vegetable stock.
- ☐ My favorite spice additions are celery seed and cayenne.

It sounds like we need to have a cook-off! Hey Moody/Bain Crew! I smell an idea (literally) for another themed get together!

2

Fairytale Ended

"The love we were promised in fairytales was never something for us to find, it has always been something for us to create."
– Tyler Kent White

Grandad, Gigi
Wes

Belinda, Alan
Venessa
Alaina
Daniel
Brenden
Teresa
Jessica
Michael, Brooke
Aubrey
Christopher, Alan, J...
Cassidy
Chloe

Nana, Pop
Corey
Marisa
Robby

"Family Names" by Daniel

Belinda – Oldest of "Original 5"

Homemaker, doula, aspiring vocalist and actress are all words and phrases to describe Belinda and the dreams she lives out. She has taught me to share in those dreams and be a sounding board for hers.

Belinda was not only dealing with becoming part of a blended family, but also became a teenage mother during this transition. She married Alan shortly after turning eighteen, when their oldest daughter was one and a half years old. Living in Georgia and engaging in a semi-crunchy lifestyle, they now have four children together: Venessa, Alaina, Daniel and Brenden.

Fishbowl Effect

Once upon a time in a place closer than you think, lived a preacher's family with five kids, a mom and a dad. The preacher's family, from this storyteller's perspective, lived in a fishbowl; always putting forth the best image possible even though sometimes that image was a façade. The kids couldn't fight, the family wasn't allowed to struggle, no one could be unhappy and no wearing shorts to church — they had to be "perfect"!

The fishbowl perspective is what happens when someone in your family is a celebrity, preacher, politician, police officer, etc. especially in a small community. Everyone seems to watch everything you do, waiting for you to screw up. We were the preacher's family — no anonymity, it was like being in a glass house.

I have always heard it said that preachers' kids and cop's kids are the worst kids, so the pressure was that much more to portray this perfection. Being interdenominational made the glass even more clear and magnifying. Everything I did was called out whether it was at school or church.

A fishbowl, though transparent, protects the inhabitants from the outside world, but when the glass shatters? Fairytale ended.

Fishbowl? An understatement! I can say this because I grew up as a preacher's kid as well. The pressure, the judgment, the looks...

No wonder we sometimes rebel. I know I did. Growing up this way helped me connect with my new stepkids. Knowing where they were coming from made things a bit easier.

Self - Blame

There were times I wondered if getting pregnant at 15 hurt my parents' marriage. Already, pain, tension, disenchantment was there, creeping in the shadows. While the king of the castle was out battling financial dragons, the queen battled the small rambunctious, almost-teleporting dragons at home.

Then, after almost 20 years of being a stay-at-home-mom, the queen got a public job of her own. The castle dynamic shifted dramatically. At 15 years old, being the oldest child and already feeling a bit like Cinderella (don't most first-borns?), I took on extra responsibilities, such as watching my younger siblings after school, fixing supper a few nights each week, etc. I do not claim to have done a good job at any of it.

The summer before my 16th birthday, my boyfriend of two years and I found out we were expecting a baby. Our news was immediately awkward, excitedly shared and sometimes vengefully proclaimed. We stood in front of our small church congregation while my father let them all know that I would be a mother in less than nine months. Some of those in attendance never returned to our church. My fault?

About a month later, my parents sat all of us kids down and explained that they would be pursuing a divorce. I felt my siblings' anger, or was it my own, turn on me, at some level, blaming me and my choices for destroying their peaceful childhood. Were they right? Sometimes, I felt we were (my siblings and me).

You hear repeatedly in life, in the movies and elsewhere, about how kids blame themselves for the divorce of their parents. Belinda's choices seemed to make this emotion even worse for her personally. The time it took her to work through this was long and hard, but she has a healthier perspective today than from before.

I have seen the statistics on teenage pregnancies, witnessed the effect on families. Some parents don't stay together, some do, some marry, some don't. Some kids grow up without fathers or end up being raised by grandparents. Some end up deep in the poverty culture with a perception of never achieving anything else.

I am happy to say Belinda and her husband, Alan, have beat the odds. They not only stayed together, they also married and today have four kids. We are proud of all they have accomplished together, the ways they have helped others and will continue to do so.

Excuses

Healing and coming together as a blended family is difficult. People will find excuses not to heal because they still haven't dealt with their pain. Excuses such as "I can't be around that person because of xyz", lack of forgiveness (which is more of a choice not an excuse), anger, lack of motivation to come halfway, etc.

More concerned with their own boo- boos instead of making things work, some parents put their wants above the needs of their children. I am not talking about issues of safety, but those of discomfort, where the adult needs to take responsibility to meet the emotional, physical, and spiritual needs of their kids. I feel angry whenever I hear these excuses from any separated or divorced parents.

Unfortunately, kids sometimes feel the brunt of excuses. We certainly went through our period of this. Belinda has been sensitive to seeing this in others. Some people end this negative cycle, others continue the excuses long term. Decide which path you will take. Consequences of either impact your sense of peace.

Keeping Everyone Happy

One of the challenges I faced was when my parents complained verbally about the other parent; I felt stuck in the middle. Being neutral was hard to do, especially with the added responsibility of my own child. I felt pulled in both directions, whether it was intentional or not.

I was in that awkward mental stage of legally being a child but having to make adult choices because of the adult choice I made in having a child at an early age. I don't know how it would have been if I had not been a teen mom, I sometimes wonder if I would have made the same choices. I found it impossible to honor both of my parents through the process. I had hurts that had been caused by the circumstances themselves. Hurts that I had to deal with and overcome.

Which way to go? Mom? Dad? Child? Child's father? Don't forget about the siblings! Belinda was overwhelmed with who to keep happy and in the end concentrated more on honoring her parents the best way she knew how while focusing on her daughter. Belinda worked her way through it all, but at times still questioned the path she took.

Unrealistic & Unmet Expectations

Timesharing between the two households and feeling like I had to choose a side seemed unrealistic to me. How do you split your time perfectly evenly? And then to be able to satisfy both sides at once? It was hard to figure out who to spend what time with. I felt I had to budget my time carefully and wisely to avoid hurt feelings, knowing my choices sometimes still hurt others.

I also had unmet expectations; I expected my parents to make it – to stay married until death. I had this ideal dream in my head that my parents' marriage was unbreakable and it would just continue – that it was shatterproof. That expectation definitely went unmet.

Idealism and reality collided and sometimes it wasn't pretty. Navigating this new world to form a new happily ever after was not always the most comfortable for Belinda. Instead she veered more into swampland rather than the walkway to the castle.

God Send

I talk about God Sends quite a bit in life because God receives credit for the "stuff" of life. My daughter, Venessa, was a God Send, even though timing looked bad. She gave me something positive to put my focus and energy into. If I had not had her, I could have turned self-destructive in actions or choices.

My stepparents are God Sends. I could have ended up with a stepmother/stepfather who was jealous of the kids' time with their spouse or was insecure with their spouse's relationship with the former spouse or even someone who was afraid of peace. This is not the case with my stepmom and stepdad.

The best advice I can give to a new or not so new stepparent is to get out of the way! I don't mean physically or even emotionally. But step back and look at the whole picture, not just the edited one you are focused on. What would be the ideal state for your blended family? All of them, not just you, your spouse and the kids. Who is hurting and how can you be a part of the solution? Insecurity and jealousy tear people apart and propel them backwards. A decision today to take steps to reverse this negative cycle will impact everyone. What small step can you start with?

Kids, no matter how old they are love their mom and dad. Okay, I am going to say that again...they <u>love their mom and dad</u>. This doesn't mean you can't be a recipient of the same kind of love. You have the opportunity to add your stepkids' lives and their parent's lives. Trust me on this one – you will reap the greatest reward in the end. ...step 1...step 2...step 3...

Prophecy of Peace

Around the same time that I received the news my childhood home had been burned beyond saving, my husband and I were trying to name our first son. I was in the third trimester, and we still didn't have a name. Our prayer was, "God, we can't figure out a name that we both like, so You have to name him." We believed God was telling us a couple of weeks later to name him Daniel Micah.

We were at church on a Sunday night, about a week later, when a visiting vocal group was singing about Jesus through the books of the Bible. The words described Jesus as the breath of life in Genesis, the rebuilder of broken lives in Nehemiah, the time and season in Ecclesiastes, the stranger in the fire in Daniel and the promise of peace in Micah.

That's when I knew, at the bottom of my soul, there was going to be peace in my family even though more than three years passed *before the first mutually peaceful get together.*

Struggling with the fire of my childhood home, struggling with the naming of our first son - both settled with a song.

I remember Belinda telling us about her confirmation. At the time peace seemed so far out of reach. We couldn't even imagine what it would look like, but we longed for it. All of us existing together and happy. How would that feel???!!

Fulfillment of Promises and Peace

The promise was fulfilled! My family has peace. We all get together, we all have a great time together. We can laugh, we can share stories about the past. We're comfortable together.

Promises can feel slow to us, but God knows that sometimes, probably most times, we will only appreciate those promises if it's been a slow-cooker-style wait. No microwave cooking in

God's timing (although He has fulfilled promises overnight for us too).

Peace, though? Peace takes time like a slow-fermenting kombucha. There are so many individual parts and pieces that need their own pace of growth and healing. If you rush it, you could destroy the work that God is doing in the secret places.

I've always heard praying for patience spells disaster. So, I never prayed for it. However, this experience has taught me patience as well as other lessons. It is so hard to wait! Today's society doesn't make us wait for much. The journey of waiting and learning is so worthwhile. Just think, if we hadn't experienced all that we have, how would we have shared our story with you?

We have peace in this family and when Belinda says we have a great time together, she does not exaggerate. As you keep reading through this book you will see all our different personalities and can imagine the beautiful chaos we make together. We love it!

Mimicking vs. Learning From

If you pay attention to fairytales, you realize many are fables; stories about what could happen when the wrong choices are made.

Cinderella's stepmom, instead of taking her under her wing and helping her through her pain, added to her pain because of jealousy and insecurity. Snow White's stepmother was so jealous of her stepdaughter that she sought to destroy her completely.

Instead of mimicking or copying these tales, we should take the lesson they present and apply it to our own lives and learn to do better ourselves. Basically, learn from other peoples' mistakes. I have seen other people make mistakes that I have learned from and thought, "Oh, that didn't work out so well, maybe I shouldn't repeat it." I also hope that others have assessed my mistakes and made efforts to do better for their stories.

May you understand this is not instant, not overnight. This isn't easy; it will sometimes hurt. The immature will find excuses and the mature will create ways. Healing will be very difficult without Jesus, for He is the healer of hearts, minds, spirits and bodies. I pray you will see this journey that has been long, but rewarding, and find hope.

I am now the oldest of a combined nine siblings. I have happy parents, no evil stepparents, healing and resolution. And the Moody/Bain family lives happily ever after...

Some learn from others, some learn the hard way on their own. All we can offer you from our story is knowledge that you are not alone. There is hope! Keep reading and know you too can have your happily ever after.

<u>Belinda's Reflections</u>

- When it comes to a blended family the parents are rarely the most important priority.

- Adult kids and minor kids are equally important in a blended family.

- Missteps, whether yours or another's can either be stumbling blocks...or stepping stones.

- Don't leave God out of it - Hold on to the promise of peace.

Belinda's Blender

Activity

Snowballs

One of my favorite memories is from my stepdad's house (when he was dating my mom). Our entire family celebrated Christmas together and one of the highlights was the "Snowball Fight."

Recipe

Peanut Butter Cereal Bars

I love to make a twist on the traditional crisped rice treat. This one is a favorite at family gatherings and came from my Mamaw Moody (Dad's mom). Peanut butter is a necessary staple in this family! No PB...end of the world. Sheesh!

Snowballs

Supplies

- ☐ White fabric cut into petal shapes
- ☐ Cotton batting/stuffing
- ☐ Bucket for snowballs
- ☐ Needle and Thread

Directions

- ☐ Sew 6 petal shapes together for each ball
- ☐ Leave a space at the top for stuffing
- ☐ Stuff each snowball with batting/stuffing
- ☐ Finish sewing hole in snowball
- ☐ Place finished snowballs in plastic pails
- ☐ Snowball Fight!

Peanut Butter Cereal Bars

Ingredients

- ☐ 3/4 cup dark Karo syrup
- ☐ 3/4 cup dark brown sugar
- ☐ 3/4 cup peanut butter
- ☐ 6 cups cereal (Cheerios, Rice Krispies, etc. -I use Honey Nut Cheerios)

Directions

- ☐ Cook Karo & brown sugar over medium heat until mixture bubbles while stirring frequently. Remove from heat.
- ☐ Add peanut butter & stir until well combined.
- ☐ Add to cereal & stir until coated.
- ☐ Press into a 13x9 pan with a buttered spatula.

3

Finding Balance - Teresa's Journey

"Imperfection is perfection."
-Flume

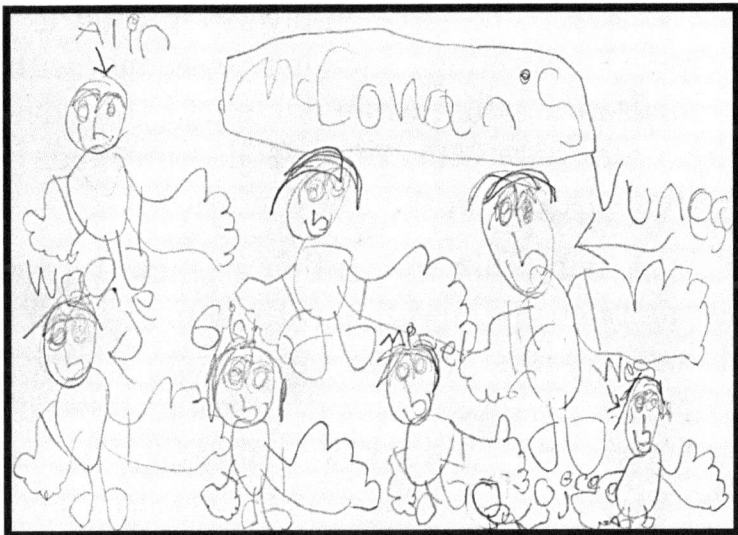

"Some of My Family" by Brenden

Teresa – #2 of "Original 5"

Adventurer, leader, teacher, world traveler and independent are all words I would use to describe Teresa. She has taught me if you listen to other people's ideas and opinions, you might just learn something! I have also discovered from her an interest in science that I never had before.

Teresa was dealing with multiple family and outside distractions as well as the new role of the oldest sibling when her older sister left home. Teresa dug into her passions with animals and nature while pursuing knowledge she could share with others. Today she holds a Master's Degree in Wildlife Studies.

A naturalist in South Carolina, Teresa has an intense connection with animals and all things outdoors. She takes us on nature walks, when we are together, and shares pictures of her creatures and their habitats. She is energetic in her role as a daughter, sister and aunt.

Foundation Crumbled

I thought I had a solid foundation, but it crumbled underneath me. I had two parents, a church, and a family. Overnight it seemed to go from one solid family unit to my parents starting to separate, then my older sister starting a new family, then issues coming up in the church, and finally the divorce.

These things happened very rapidly and my beliefs of what was true completely changed. Suddenly we became the bare bones of what human social structure is. We were a bunch of people trying to make it in the world, not as a solidified group, but as a bunch of moving parts.

Teresa, a natural leader, took on the new role as the oldest of her siblings as well as protector of her family from the outside world. She was attempting to bring the pieces together but instead the perplexity of two households, her leadership role, school and work engulfed her.

Distractions and Conversations

Distractions of family issues, work, school, a new baby brother, etc. kept me from dealing with my emotions and probably prolonged me gaining my bearings on the direction our family had taken. I felt like it took me a long time to deal with everything, nearly ten years to be exact. Paying attention to the distractions instead of dealing with my emotions and reality was my coping mechanism.

The reality was very difficult for me to deal with because it was so painful. The seemingly endless discussions and outbursts angered and confused me more than helped me. It seemed like we were talking but never really communicating. I wasn't honing in on what was happening on a day to day basis. I experienced a lot of emotion and turmoil and not a lot of focus. There was a lot of venting on both sides, a lot of pointing fingers, a lot of judgment. Rather than focusing on fixing what the problems were, we talked about each *other's particular issues. This dynamic was so starkly different from what the family was before, where there was love and support and rare angry outbursts. Now, the clear communication was rare.*

Even though it was rare, I appreciated direct, guiding conversations and would cave under a negative influence. Anytime there was name calling or finger pointing from my parents (who had been so supportive of each other during their marriage) or anytime they would do something completely out of character from who I thought them to be, it would shatter me. I probably had an unhealthy ideal perception of who they were and thought of them as this overly supporting and loving married couple. To see the opposite destroyed me. In turn, I would have outbursts, disappear and be angry. I didn't want to be around the people who were causing me pain.

Sometimes it is easier to focus on distractions or the things you can control in your life, even though you want to fix what you can't control. The phrase "Time heals all wounds" has a word that we sometimes forget – "Time." Teresa needed time to process the changes and emotions surrounding her. Her coping mechanism of focusing on the distractions of life prolonged her healing process, yes, but we all have different ways of dealing with situations. Solutions can't be cookie cutter for everyone. As you are helping your family muddle through the confusion, remember, there is no wrong way to process. Leave judgment for judges who are voted to the bench. Instead, patience and love will prevail.

When things are not working in a blended family, it is frustrating. You want it to be the way it was and when it is not, you don't understand. Why do people make things messy instead of solving the problem? We are human. We have feelings. We hurt. Logic doesn't always have a voice in these situations. Teresa focused her energy on trying to "fix" the family, but the issues were more than anyone could handle at the time.

Quality Time

Leading up to the divorce my dad was considered somewhat absent because of traveling through the week due to his job. Dad changed jobs and after the divorce, he was very present. It was a total paradigm shift. Dad cooking for us was a new and weird thing. This meant a lot of burger nights and cinnamon toast mornings, but it did show he was trying to create some semblance of what we had before. We had more burgers, fries, pizza, movie nights and together time than we maybe had before which maintained a strong feeling of love even through the chaos.

The same happened with Mom. Before Dad was the repairman and after, it was up to Mom and me to maintain the house. I have distinct memories of moving a washing machine and cutting the grass together. Not that those things didn't happen before, but after the divorce, she and I had to become a team. I was responsible for a lot more. I wound up getting jobs to try and take some burden off both of my parents financially. It was not an easy thing and I would not recommend having three jobs at 15 years old, but I did learn a lot during that time.

Previous family roles typically change when a household of one becomes two. Sometimes a person plays the same role and sometimes they do not.

Teresa's dad, Wayne, became a "chef" and today has many family favorite recipes. In fact, he cooks way more than I do. Cooking was never my thing because I like things very organized, prepped in advance and I follow recipes to the "T". In a large family, this does not always work. You will find it necessary to cook on the fly and Wayne does just that. If it can't be prepared in less than 30 minutes, then this man does not fool with it.

Teresa's mom, Pam, became a "home repair specialist" and to date has conquered many home maintenance and remodel projects and we are not just talking painting here, people. One of the benefits of a big family, is there are many hands to help. I am still amazed at the things Pam did to her house she sold earlier this year after she and John married and became one household. John helped as well, but Pam has some bragging rights.

Teresa is a person who takes the lead and jumps in to get the job done. She felt it was her duty to be a front-runner for the family. Kids will grow and learn during these difficult transition periods. Take this opportunity to foster their independence. They will be successful adults because of the experience.

Therapy

I immediately got the farthest from my dad and stayed closer to my mom. I pulled away from my dad for personal reasons. We were mad at each other. I felt like I had lost my father during the divorce and I think he felt like he lost me.

I wanted to attempt trying to have a dad again. I felt the best way to do this at the time was with a mediator to talk things out. It happened too soon. Raw emotions came out and the mediator did not mediate. Instead, it turned ugly. We both got upset and Dad yelled at me and didn't believe my side of things. The therapist did nothing in response. It was the most disappointing moment I've ever experienced with a medical professional. It was possibly the lowest point with Dad as well. I pulled further away from him for a long time. We did not continue therapy sessions after that. I did realize that the therapist was simply not a good professional, and I did pursue therapy later.

Therapy can be a helpful tool for healing. In this case, it made things a little worse between Teresa and her dad. I remember seeing them both hurting and heartbroken. They still loved each other, but getting through the toughness of the situation was difficult. It is important to keep a connection even when you are not in agreement during a period like this one. Keep trying, keep reaching out in small ways. Eventually, the wholeness you once had will return.

Understanding the Humanity of My Parents

As a teen, I was damaged and it has taken me a very long time to be understanding. Trying to cope with what the divorce meant as well as also comprehending and appreciating what my parents did and why was difficult. I have always loved them for who they are, even if I didn't agree, but going that one step further and trying to grasp the human reason behind it, was tough for me and beyond my capability at the time.

Adulthood and time have helped me to realize my parents are human and that is why they do the things they do. That is why I do the things I do. My perfect perceived image of my parents was an unhealthy ideal of who they really were. Attempting to comprehend their choices has allowed me to be closer to them but I don't think it is a necessary step for everyone. However, it was a necessary step for me.

Until I accepted my parents' limitations, their humanness, and the ugliness, I was still angry. The propensity of all of us to make mistakes causes friction with those we love the most. With time and healing on both parts, I accepted the conflict in therapy between my dad and me because it was not a continued pattern, but a one-time thing.

Through this journey, I have always loved and supported my parents, but something else had to take place. The answer was forgiveness and forgiveness has released me.

Understanding is developed over time and after a thoughtful process of empathy for how others are. Perception is different for everyone and we may truly never know exactly how a person feels or what they have experienced. We all exhibit life in amazing ways which lends itself to the diversity we know. Otherwise, our existence would be monotonous.

Forgiveness is freeing for both mind and spirit. Forgiveness takes time and brings peace to the chaos of tough situations. What is out of order in your life? What emotions are keeping you from moving forward? Is there someone you need to forgive so that you can soar?

Teresa has a healthy view of her parents now; no pedestal approach in the way she sees them. She still may not comprehend all their choices, but she does understand that they are human, just as she is, and she loves them and the way they love her.

Self-Reflection

With immense love from my family and some professional help from a great therapist, I realized and corrected the damage in myself. The only way I fully processed and dealt with my coping mechanisms was through self-reflection. My daily worldly perception was affected by me not confronting my emotions. I solved my problems and filtered this skewed view of everything I encountered through an unhealthy lens.

With my therapist's help, I learned to no longer respond by shutting down and going into a "zombie-like" state. I had to understand and combat my coping mechanisms. She helped me to be able to handle my emotions and use tools to make the relationships with my family better.

We never stop learning. Recognizing who we are and how we respond is only half of the struggle. We have a choice, to move forward or to regress into a state of defeat, thereby never dealing with our emotions. Teresa chose to move forward, to guide her feelings, to mend the relationships with her family.

Great is the reward of self-reflection and mastering our life experiences. Everything we engage in forms our base, our foundation. The journey we take is what makes us who we are. Think back on the steps you have chosen in your path. What has life offered you? How have you responded and what choices have you made? How has your journey made you who you are?

Backpacking with Dad

On a trip about three years ago, I went backpacking with my dad. That is where I felt like our relationship came full circle. We had adult discussions, where I no longer felt he saw me as a child or a wounded duckling, but instead as an independent adult. He asked me questions and we even discussed hot topics that I knew we wouldn't agree on. At that point, I knew there was enough healing for us to become close again.

This was different from the dad I knew during the divorce. The trip, with just the two of us, laid the groundwork to what we have today and helped me to realize my dad is a person I really like being around.

It is important for a parent to have special time with their kids, even when they are adults. You never know what barriers can be removed or memories can be made when this happens. Be open to the views of the other person when talking about subjects you don't agree on. Listening and discussing, even if you agree to disagree, shows an interest and respect which establishes the foundation for continual connection.

I was the one who picked up Teresa and her dad after their backpacking trip of two days. They were happy and a little stinky, but I could tell something had changed between them. They experienced everything from seeing who could identify the most trees to sleeping in a rock shelter and taking precautions to not attract bears. I listened to them recap their trip excitedly as I took them back to the beginning place of their trek to pick up Teresa's car. Once again, I was privileged to witness restoration in this family. And it continues to improve all the time.

Regained Footing

The world slid out from under me, but I regained my footing. Instead of one solid foundation, there are a lot of moving parts. I had to figure out how and why things work,

*why things were the way they were. My family
fell apart and came back together. Even
though the pieces fit differently now, the
structure seems to have improved. I have
improved as well.*

Teresa had a challenging journey; maybe yours is the same, maybe it is different. She sought to understand and lost ground amid the muck. Finding her place once again, she came full circle with her emotions and responses, thereby rebuilding relationships with her loved ones. Her family is a variation of what it previously was, but underneath it all remains genuine love.

<u>Teresa's Reflections</u>

- Whatever can be broken, can be fixed through time and effort.

- The repair may not look like what we expect; it may be even better.

- Outbursts of emotion and pretending everything is okay prolongs forgiveness and healing.

- Just because everything is moving doesn't mean you can't find sure footing.

- Genuine love can provide the foundation for healing.

Teresa's Blender

Activity

Blended Family Nature Walks

I think being outside and having "free play" is very important for children. Since there are many children in our family, I think this is one of the favorite activities for everyone. I engage them in looking for animals or just enjoying the environment around them. Kids will naturally find games to play or ways to engage with each other in more energetic ways.

This is a great way to get group and one-on-one time. Exercising together also increases endorphins and encourages bonding.

Recipe

Snickerdoodles

I am often asked to make these snickerdoodles at family functions. This recipe was given to my mother from her German neighbor lady when she was a little girl.

It's impossible to resist eating these as they come out of the oven. They are also delicious with coffee or chocolate milk.

Teresa's Nature Walks

Supplies

- ☐ The Great Outdoors

Directions

- ☐ Pick a favorite trail or even just the backyard.

- ☐ Explore together! Discuss and share what you find with each other.

- ☐ Find a game to play or come up with a challenge for the group.

- ☐ Challenge Ideas:

- ☐ Who can skip a rock the farthest?

- ☐ Who can find the prettiest flower/rock/etc.? (follow all applicable guidelines about collection of natural objects)

- ☐ Make animals out of leaves.

- ☐ Make stick houses.

Teresa's Snickerdoodles

Ingredients

- ☐ 1 cup shortening
- ☐ 1 ½ cup sugar
- ☐ 2 eggs
- ☐ 2 ¾ cup flour
- ☐ 1 teaspoon baking soda
- ☐ 2 teaspoons cream of tartar
- ☐ ½ teaspoon salt
- ☐ Sugar
- ☐ Cinnamon

Directions

- ☐ Preheat oven to 400 degrees.
- ☐ Mix the first 3 ingredients. Set aside.
- ☐ Sift the flour, baking soda, cream of tartar, and salt together.
- ☐ Slowly add the dry ingredients to the wet ingredients. Blend well. Chill the dough until firm.

☐ Mix a ratio* of 3 tablespoons sugar & 1 tablespoon cinnamon in a small bowl. Place a small amount on a plate.

☐ Roll the dough into 1-1 ½ inch balls. Evenly coat the dough balls in the cinnamon-sugar mixture.

☐ Place dough on a parchment paper lined cookie sheet 1-2 inches apart.

☐ Bake for 8-10 minutes until the top cracks and the edges are golden brown.

*This ratio is my best guess. I just mix the two until the mixtures "look right".

This recipe makes about 36 cookies.

4

Chaotic Support

"The hardest thing about being a blended family is knowing when to fight and knowing when to let it go."
-Unknown

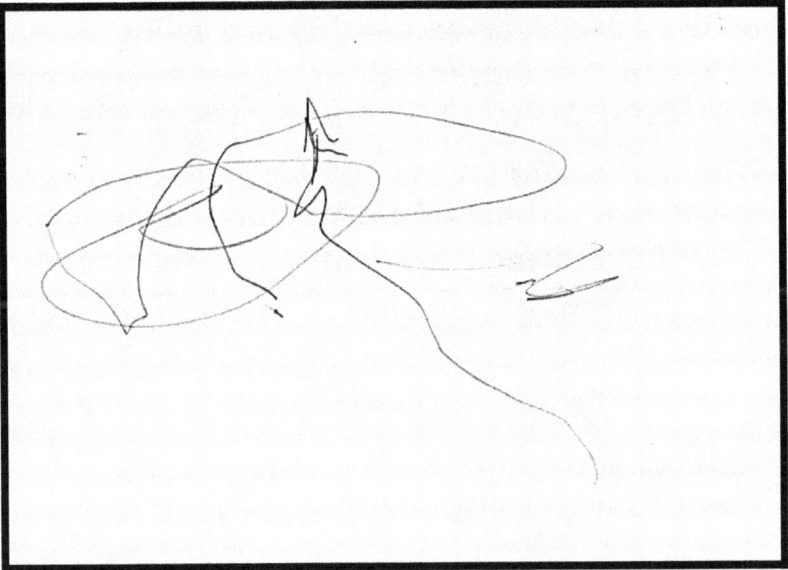

"We Were Sad and Now We Are Happy" by Cassidy

(also for her sister Chloe, who is too little to draw)

JAYNE – #3 of "Original 5"

Homemaker, photographer, soccer player, devoted and dry/hilarious humor are all words I would use to describe Jayne. She has taught me to be open to expressions of disagreement without the consequences of rejection. I have also learned not to take life so seriously and that there is always room for laughter from many sources.

Jayne was dealing with the beginnings of being a teenager as well as struggling with judgment from others. Becoming a strong and successful soccer player through high school and beyond was part of how she dealt with the turmoil around her. Her dry humor, to this day, always makes me laugh and can lift me up in a way that makes whatever I am dealing with seem trivial.

Living in Texas, Jayne is married to Christopher Alan, who is in the military, and they have two daughters, Cassidy and Chloe.

Tougher than Tough

Being a new teen is tough enough, but I had to be tougher than tough. When my teen years hit, my family was splitting apart. Others around me seemed somewhat carefree, except about school, but they didn't have all this going on.

I became numb to a lot of it, sometimes ignoring it, and played soccer instead of thinking about the changes and what was going on. Soccer provided for me a team of girls that didn't know what I was dealing with at home and didn't really care. I could go there and not have to focus on my family's situation. Soccer was an escape for me.

Some of my favorite memories of Jayne were during soccer games. She always had this tenacious attitude as she conversed loudly with her teammates all the way down the field. I imagined her mind playing over and over, "Ball, ball, ball" as she constantly focused her foot skills towards easing the ball into a scoring position as if a flip of her foot would send it to the perfect spot. She never stopped, following through until the last blow of the whistle. Seeing her dedication impacted the way I look at following through on one's words and actions.

Focusing on soccer was a positive way for Jayne to handle the challenges of a new blended family, and her devotion to the sport allowed her to become an excellent defensive player. Helping kids to find a focus outside of the day to day challenges will strengthen their character and provide an outlet for them to escape to.

Judgment

Judgment from the community, people in the church, people who were close to us was one of the hardest things to deal with. "Oh, your parents are divorced, so you know where you are going!" People would bring up details that they shouldn't have known about, things they shouldn't have said to me, things they shouldn't have been gossiping about. Truth isn't always what people believe and it's certainly not always what they repeat.

Judgment from others makes you feel pretty crappy especially when it is people who are close to you. I questioned what I was learning in church versus what other people were saying. I attended different churches with friends trying to learn which biblical teachings were right and which were wrong. I finally concluded that no one sin is worse than another sin. God looks at all sin the same, and He forgives.

My parents forgave each other...and I forgave my parents... and I forgave those whose judgment added to our heartbreak.

As outsiders, we don't always realize how our words and actions affect others. We live in our little world and the people around us sometimes become our "entertainment". The next time you feel the need to criticize or just "discuss" a situation you are not a part of, please think about how what you say may hurt more than help.

Forgiveness is more for yourself than for other people and sometimes when you forgive, you don't necessarily tell the person you have forgiven...and sometimes you do. Holding in those negative emotions allows someone else to have control over you and if you think about it, they probably are completely unaware of how they affect you. Forgive, let it go, be free to focus on peace in your life rather than the disorder.

Life Isn't Cookie Cutter

We were so sheltered, only one school, only one town, Christian USA. Everybody's parents married, or so we thought, no blended families... and then I get these stepparents. I learned quickly everybody is not the same.

So, when I was thrown these two oddballs, it was eye opening. We had put all families in a box like us, but there were other families, other ways of doing things, other priorities. Different families had other goals, other ways of disciplining, even different movies they would see...other ways of being a family.

Adjustment is always part of becoming a blended family. Imagine a kid whose life has an expected rhythm and then, "Bam", is now a part of two households. Dealing with new adults in a parental role, whose personalities are foreign to them, is difficult at best.

Be patient as everyone adjusts to the new household members and new schedules. Keeping the majority of old routines and periodically introducing new activities will make the transition easier.

Jealousy

At first it felt like my parents were putting the new spouses first. Going on trips with their new spouse when we were at the other household would make me feel left behind. Decisions that were made putting the spouses first, felt like they were choosing them, not us. Felling like they were talking to or treating us differently from before, adding another sibling even though there were already five of us, was hard to understand.

By the time my new little brother was born, I was past my jealous feelings and besides that, he was just a baby. The focus of attention changed because it had to, we had different members of our family now. To an extent, we were robbed of having that together family, robbed of those few years of just our original family. Now it's one little family, another little family, and then us kids...we have a tribe of parents now and added siblings. It's just different from before.

Quality time between biological parents and their children is important as well as forging a strong bond between the new couple. Build foundations to provide lasting relationships that will weather the storms ahead. Carve out special time for the kids to be with their bio parent, their stepparent and as a together family. Make sure the parental couples are spending time together as well. Sometimes this will seem awkward, but consistent time spent pays off in the long run.

Jayne's signature color was pink during her teenage years. She and her dad dressed up and went out on a father/daughter date night, both accented in her favorite shade. They would also practice soccer foot skills in the backyard together. I became quite familiar with mall shopping as Jayne and I plunged into the world of teenage clothes.

We ended up unexpectedly adding another sibling, Wes, to the "Original 5". Shifting from taking care of a newborn while still supporting the kid's activities was a bit chaotic at times. Wes is almost 20 years younger than his oldest sibling and almost 10 years younger than his youngest sibling. He also has two nieces who are older than him and now has five nieces and nephews' younger than him. Wes is the only child I have given birth to, so...., new mom, ongoing stepmom, all requiring a physical and mental strength I had never needed to engage before.

One soccer game, scheduled during school hours, was impossible for both of Jayne's parents to attend due to their traveling work schedules. Wes, at approximately three months old, and I followed behind the bus to see Jayne play. Thankfully he was a baby who would journey wherever his siblings needed to go. We did everything together as a family, despite the challenges.

Tension / Frustration

My parents would sometimes fight like middle school children and create tension like boiling water flowing out of a pan. Seeing this was frustrating.

Scheduling events and time together and figuring out what each kid was doing, where they were going, was always difficult. We had to coordinate many schedules between two households. Three of us played soccer, one of us was very involved in school organization activities and the other had started a family of her own.

When I was in high school and old enough to drive my younger siblings to their soccer practices, working with both parents was not always easy. Making sure everyone was where they were supposed to be and feeling like I was the middle man going back and forth between them, proved challenging at times because at that point they weren't really talking to each other.

We as parents are not always the best at dealing with difficult situations. We sometimes put others in the middle of dealing with our responsibilities. Emotions run high at times and adding to the situation with our own quirkiness makes it harder for our kids to deal with the already overwhelming frustration they feel. Are we perfect at this? No!

I could see the kids shut down whenever communication between the households was difficult. All of us shared in some of the guilt in this. This isn't easy; we screwed it up too! Back when things were tense between the households, we all were frustrated in our own way. In the end, what we have now has taken away the sting of the past. Little by little you can get to this point too. Be encouraged and don't expect overnight success. We all have walls that need chipping away and sometimes all we have is a butter knife.

Anti-Boring

Our family is already what you would call...anti-boring? My mom has three sisters; my dad has three brothers. Our extended family gatherings seem to always have about 20 billion people with 20 billion conversations. Multiple stories involving many personalities, lots of food and never a dull moment. "Oh, you have a new job? Oh, three months ago?"

Each side would have things to say about the other side to some extent. As a young teenager, I was trying to figure out how my parents and stepparents are themselves and then "hearing" well, you know, how they "really" are or how their family is.

My stepmom, Georgie, added to this anti-boring state. She brought experiences into our family that were very different - -the food, the traditions, her family, being so overly affectionate that it was almost uncomfortable because our family wasn't like that. Having a hugger for a stepmom was awkward for me in the beginning.

Navigating through all of this made life less boring...kind of like watching a bunch of squirrels jumping on a trampoline.

Knowing how to show affection in your new family can be challenging and awkward until you know how others will react. I am definitely the hugging type and had to figure out how the kids expressed their emotions when it wasn't as physical as what I did. We all adapted. They hug more now, and I hug a little less. We understand the non-verbal and non-physical cues of expression as well.

Letting People In – Be Open Minded

We went from a single- family setting to adding these other people. I didn't feel I really had enough time to get to know them, even though it was more than a year before they married into the family. I was at a sensitive time for trust during that period. Trust these people I felt like I just met? And now I am just letting them in?

When opposites mix in a blended family there will still be periods of uneasiness until you figure out how to make it work. Keep trying. Eventually you will find that middle ground and in the meantime, your experiences with each other prepare you for dealing with others who are not like you.

Before you read this next part, please visualize someone you know with a dry humor to have the full effect of Jayne's hilarious words. When I was writing this book, this paragraph made me laugh multiple times.

Tradition!

I remember when my stepmom tried to feed us eggplant for the first time. "Has this woman lost her mind? What was she thinking? Is she trying to kill us!?" I saw it more at that time as her trying to change things instead of it being interesting, as her weird and different food is now.

Once or twice a year, I would feast on my favorite holiday food which was, to me, normal, comforting, traditional...the way food was supposed to be. Tradition makes me think of a melody from a play about someone playing on the top of a house. At first it was a bit offensive because everything was new, but later and with time we all adjusted and are now comfortable with our differences from both sides. We all adapted to each other in a good way.

I love this perspective! Jayne was dealing with my weirdness as much as I was dealing with it too. I grew up in a family who was always different, stood out in the crowd and never stayed in one place too long. Change was the constant state of my life. Mixing this lifestyle with a more structured family, that included five kids, was intriguing at times and challenging always.

Something about their father and the lot of them made me want to scoop them all up. They had all grabbed my heart in a way I had never felt before. I was in love with a man and loved his five kids too. What was this? Bad eggplant? I loved their mother as well...now I knew I was crazy! Seeing them restored back together as a successfully blended family, with all our extras, is a utopia for me. Call me nutty; I'm okay with it. God knew I needed this man, these kids, their mom and all that goes with it to balance my own personality. I love this family!!!

Chaotic Support

With five kids and many activities, life was hectic. Part of the reason our support was chaotic was that it was always a toss-up as to where it was coming from. We could count on our family to champion us, sometimes in a positive way or with constructive criticism, but the consistency was there.

Even though everything was chaotic, somebody was there, somebody cared. I always had somebody at every event, soccer game, field trip, etc. that I was participating in. I witnessed other kids who didn't have that kind of sustainability and sometimes it was hard for them to keep playing.

One Saturday, my two younger siblings and I all had soccer games at the same time, in three completely different areas. My parents and stepmom divided up to cover those games.

Life is crazy in a blended family, but one thing you can provide in the craziness is to be an advocate for your kids even when the separate households are not getting along. We ran around everywhere, all of us, trying our best to make sure the kids had someone there, someone familiar and who would go to bat for them that they could see in the crowd of faces. Sometimes it was quiet support, sometimes loud. Sometimes peaceful, sometimes tense. But always there.

Moving Forward

With all the different people, my family has taught me many things I wanted to do with my kids and my marriage. It taught me things I wanted to do and not want to do, so I learned from that. I know what healthy versus unhealthy relationships look like. I know what to watch for and what to strive for. I am not judged if I want to ask questions.

Now everyone blends and is not hateful to each other. Our family dynamic is easier now, where it used to be uncomfortable and stressful. Everybody has grown up and worked through their emotions. Considering the love and backing I have been surrounded with, I would never change my outcome. Our large happy gatherings now bring us peace that can only be compared to the feeling of a fresh spring morning.

Everything can fall in place, but everyone has their own pace and their own expectations. Trust the process and take those small steps towards progress. If the desire is there, you will all change. Hopefully, it is for the better. If the desire is not there, then wait for the opportunity. It's amazing what time will do to the past.

<u>Jayne's Reflections</u>

- Be supportive of the entire family, not just the side you choose to be friends with after they are no longer one household.

- Don't pass judgment on your perception of whatever the family is dealing with and in turn gossip about it.

- An outsider, no matter how close they are to the family, doesn't know everything that everyone is dealing with.

- Be as helpful as possible in everyday life responsibilities while the parents are figuring out their emotions, next steps and just life in general. Sometimes all they need is help in picking the kids up from soccer practice.

Jayne's Blender

Activity

Family Photo Day

Supporting a local budding photographer, by hiring them to take pictures, is a great way to capture family memories. Spending time together at a park and having fun, even better!

Recipe

Jayne's Peach Cobbler

My version of peach cobbler. Yum!

Family Photo Day

Supplies

- ☐ Hobby Photographer or Local Budding Photographer
- ☐ Family
- ☐ Picnic
- ☐ Park
- ☐ Field Day Supplies

Directions

- ☐ Hire a hobby or local budding photographer.
- ☐ Pack a picnic.
- ☐ Go to a local park.
- ☐ Set up family field day.
- ☐ Have fun while the photographer takes pictures!

Jayne's Peach Cobbler

Ingredients

- ☐ 1 box of Jiffy Yellow Cake Mix
- ☐ 1 stick of melted butter
- ☐ 2 cans of sliced peaches (or 1 large can)

Directions

- ☐ Preheat oven to 350 degrees.
- ☐ Pour peaches in 8x8 or 9x9 pan.
- ☐ Melt butter and mix with cake mix.
- ☐ Pour over peaches.
- ☐ Bake until lightly brown on top (30-45 minutes).

5

Michael's Amazing, Fantastic, Terrific, Wonderful Story

"Some families are created in different ways but are still in every way a family."
-Unknown

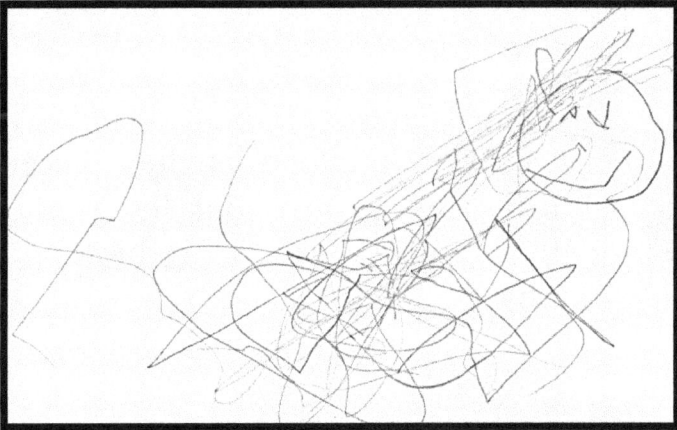

"Mommy and Daddy" by Audrey
(with a little help from Alaina)

MICHAEL- #4 of "Original 5"

Outdoorsy, provider, an uncle who is a big kid, goofy humor, soccer player, quirky and social are all words I would use to describe Michael. He has taught me to be supportive of him without trying to insert my agenda. I have also learned to love and respect our family, quirks and all, because I also have quirks that are weird.

Michael was dealing with his role as the new "man of the house" as well as learning some things the "hard way." Embracing his love of the outdoors and physical activity helped him connect with his emotions and those around him.

Living in Tennessee, Michael is married to Brooke, and they have one daughter, Audrey. Michael loves his family, and his younger brother thinks he is the best big brother he could ever have.

Wedding

A boy, with a spoiled, jealous heart didn't want to hold a ring. My dad was getting married. I told him I would be his best man, but I was mad because he was marrying someone else, someone who wasn't my mom. I said yes at the last minute. I just let go of the anger and jealousy for my dad's sake. I didn't feel it at the time, but now I have a bigger and better family.

Michael had a hard time adjusting to his parents' remarrying. Wayne and I were married first and we could see Michael struggling with being a part of the wedding. The girls were my bridesmaids and Michael did end up being the best man, but at the last minute. I still remember him coming up to me at the house after the wedding and looking at me with a sideways glance and saying, "Mom? Nah...just George!" (Most of the kids call me George, rather than Georgie.) I never had a desire to replace his mom, just add to his life as "George".

I made a public vow at the wedding to my new stepkids, to love them and support them and to love their father. Their stepdad, John, made a similar vow to them and their mom, Pam, made a similar vow to her new stepkids earlier this year. In this family, all kids are "our kids". Time has proven the dedication we all have to each other.

Bubble Popped

I had to learn to accept that my parents can be wrong. We lived in this perfect sheltered little world as preacher's kids. I remember in the second grade someone had told me the "f" word. So, I went around all day repeating it because I had never heard it and didn't know it was bad. In our family, nobody did anything wrong; people looked up to us, people looked up to my parents. Then one day, some people started to look down instead of up. I was sad and scared. My bubble popped.

I don't remember my parents fighting. It surprised me when they told us, during the month of my birthday, they were separating. Bad timing. After the separation, I started to notice the cracks and fissures in their relationship, even though I didn't want to see it. The first time I heard them being ugly to each other, I went to my room and cried for an hour.

Kids have an image of their parents at a young age that sometimes is not reality. This is called "Hero Vision". Don't get me wrong, it's okay for your parents to be your heroes. Our youngest son, Wes, told me while I was writing this book that I had super hero powers because I was a mom and a stepmom. There are times, I still believe my dad is faster than a speeding bullet and can leap tall buildings in a single bound. Not reality, but it's still cool to think about.

Kids never need to be in the middle of disagreements, but they do need to see that you can have discussions, disagree, still love each other and function in a relationship. We are all human and have issues to overcome. Growing together and helping kids to grow along with you sets the tone for future relationships. Sometimes it doesn't work out as you see here, but in the long term it did. We just have a different set of relationships from before.

Fear of Being Replaced

Understanding my parents weren't abandoning us for other people was a big challenge for me. The divorce happened when I was very young, not even a teenager yet, and so I didn't realize we were so separated. The two households were only a few miles from each other. We still had a good situation due to spending time with my dad every other weekend, every other Wednesday, half the holidays, half of school breaks and with my mom the rest of the time. My wife, who also came from a blended family situation, dealt with multiple weekends where she didn't even see her dad.

I still had issues with jealousy. My parents would go out with their spouses when we were with the other parent and even though I didn't want to go on these "dates", I was still jealous. Maturity taught me that they didn't want someone more than me, they were just spending time that I didn't understand then.

We still spent time doing family activities together.

Before the divorce and when we were younger, we would go camping a lot as a family. I remember with longing and sadness the fire crackling in the woods and the leaves beneath our feet. Now it was separate. Now we were with just Mom. Now we were with just Dad. My parents were not together anymore and I feared being replaced.

Finding a balance of spending time with the kids as a new couple, letting them spend time with just their dad or just me and spending alone time with my husband was challenging. We tried to maximize time with the kids when they were with us, so I can only remember one "date" we went on without them and that ended up being a church event they weren't interested in attending at the time. Our "dates" were mostly when the kids were with their mom, but we still scheduled lots of family time when they were with us. Again, though, perception is different with everyone.

Michael was dealing with a loss of his family and new stepparents weren't a part of the way he wanted things. Remember the statistic from the first chapter referencing kids having a harder time with a parent's remarriage rather than the divorce of biological parents? On the outside, Michael seemed mostly adjusted, but occasionally we would see him express himself otherwise.

Continued support and patience is sometimes the only way to deal with a kid who is jealous and fears replacement. Michael was never disrespectful towards me, we have always had a good relationship. I did have to ground him once, and he accepted it. Neither of us can remember the details of why, but we do laugh about it, since I never had to ground his sisters.

Connections

Our first night back at Dad's house, after picking us up in his big red truck, typically meant pizza night, which was something we didn't eat all the time. Pizza would set the mood for the weekend along with the fun stuff to do outside the house like playing in the treehouse, jumping on the trampoline, basketball, volleyball, building something or just kicking around a soccer ball. Some summer nights we would all relax around on the deck eating Dad's hamburgers after a day of playing and working outside.

My stepmom, Georgie, made enchiladas and they were good. Anything with beef and cheese was considered comfort food. Even though it was new, the food at Dad's house was still the same general quality of food as a home cooked meal where everybody sat down and ate together, just like at Mom's house. Different house, different family context but still my family. I had two households to connect with rather than one.

Connecting around activities and food seems natural in a family. It's a part of everyday life. The kids had experiences in both households they didn't have before and they still had a semblance of some of the ways life used to be. All of it was new and old and different all at the same time. How confusing! Sorting out the way they felt was sometimes an inner struggle and sometimes expressed outwardly.

We ate a lot of pizza, where at their mom's house they had more home cooked meals. The shared experience, however, was eating together as a new family, even though now we were separate.

Life Outdoors

Pure joy and excitement for me was playing outside in the sun, feeling and smelling the sweat on my skin. I didn't worry about anything; I was too young to care. All I knew about was playing with my siblings and other kids, working on projects with my dad, spending time with my mom, and just being a kid.

As I got older, a state of melancholy would settle over me as I walked through the woods by myself and over the rocks in the creek bed. I was bored at times and would think more about the issues in my family and by then understood more of what was going on. Feeling sad and lonely, I longed for a way to make sense of the whole thing.

I thought about what it would be like when I grew up. I would have a big truck and a treehouse. I would build manly stuff, put things together...I would be happy.

Michael still connects more with the outdoors rather than inside. He was a young kid when his parents divorced, not yet a teenager. I like to tease him about having pictures to prove he was once shorter than me back when he also had a squeaky voice. He is now about 6' 3" tall and his voice is deeper than his dad's. He can make heads turn with that voice.

Playing with his siblings or the neighbor kids was more fun to Michael than dealing with the issues of his new family situation. As he got older, things became clearer, but still didn't make him feel better. Instead of escaping to his room, which he often did, he opted more for the escape of the outdoors. He longed to make things better for himself in adulthood.

Contradictions Like a Pendulum

I was always smart, but stubborn. I didn't care about school and would make bad grades. Dad would say "You can do it, you are better than this." So, I wouldn't do it just because Dad said to. If I had just realized years before and had not been so stubborn, life would be a whole lot easier now. But, I had to learn the hard way.

Everyone will have an opinion – you will agree, disagree, argue or yell. When you push something away from yourself, you are also pushing away from that which you are trying to get closer to. Sometimes you must pull things in; otherwise, you are hurting yourself. When you move something forward, you must step back to brace yourself. But, if you are constantly pushing forward, you are not allowing things to come to you, like a pendulum. Dad and I disagreed because I just wanted to disagree.

Sometimes you have a better way of doing something, but sometimes you need to quit being so stubborn and just do what you need to do. Don't be afraid to contradict others or, more importantly, yourself.

Yes, Michael had to learn the hard way on most things. I get this because I was one of those kids too. Does this make it harder for people like us? Definitely!

Be careful in guiding someone who is stubborn. Helping them to talk it out without inserting your own agenda is best. Hopefully, they will make the right decisions, most of the time they do, sometimes not. But they must always own their decision.

We stubborn people can learn, and hopefully, others can learn from our mistakes. Eventually, we get tired of being so stubborn and improve our listening skills, but we still want to do things the way we think is best. At least now we are open to listening to other opinions and occasionally, we apply those opinions to our own situation.

Figuring it All Out

For a while, when Dad first had his own place, I slept in the living room on a futon when we were at his house. I helped Dad eventually build in a room that was mine. My sisters already had their own rooms. My new room had tile that looked like rock stone and was cool to the touch. The new room allowed me space of my own to think about deciding how life was going to be with the separate families and a new baby brother. I was trying to figure it all out.

There was a small amount of jealousy towards my new brother. At times, when I felt like I was dealing with things that were "stupid", it would annoy me. I didn't understand he was just a little kid. When you feel like you must cater to people around you and it annoys you, you get tired of it.

Everything becomes annoying. Everything gets on your nerves.

I didn't feel like I was always a great older brother. I was catering to a scenario I didn't want to cater to. He had opportunities that we didn't have. It was supposed to be about me, not him. I have a lot of regret about the way I treated my little brother. I should have been more kind.

Annoyance ties in with jealousy. It was a misunderstanding, not reality. It wasn't one or the other, I just couldn't see it at the time. I realized it wasn't necessarily about anyone. Now I am old enough to understand the differences. We were all catered to.

Michael and I discussed this topic when writing his chapter for the book. I was surprised at how deeply he felt about his past role in his brother's life versus now. Wes adores Michael and looks up to him in the way most younger brothers do to their older brothers. Thirteen years separate the two and so, you can see how a little kid would be annoying to a teenager, especially when that little kid needs more attention until he can do more things on his own.

We left Wes with Michael to take a "quick" grocery trip while Wes was still in diapers and old enough to get around on his own. Returning to the house, we noticed Michael had changed his shirt, Wes was wearing a backwards diaper and the sofa cushion was gone. "Hmmm...what happened, Michael?" You can guess about the blowout Wes had without me getting into all the details. Michael took care of his younger brother in the best way he knew how to at the time.

Today, I watch Michael with his daughter and the way he takes care of her, feeds her, changes her, deals with the "messy" stuff of having a kid. His experiences of having a younger brother and nieces and nephews have turned him into a great dad. He is aware of how he affects these little people around him. He plays with them because he is a big kid himself. We are proud of him and love him immensely.

Admit and Accept Being Wrong

Learning to admit and accept being wrong was my most painful moment. I didn't want to like my parents. I didn't want to like Georgie. My parents aren't perfect and they don't necessarily know what they are doing all the time. My painful moment of truth was in figuring out that my mom and dad were not going to be together anymore. If I wanted to see Dad, I had to go see Dad. If I wanted to see Mom, I had to go see Mom.

Now things are different. I can't imagine my parents together except as what they are now, which is as friends. They have both grown in separate directions and are both better people because of it.

Ever heard the phrase, "Kids are resilient"? They are, to some extent. A split family will still affect them. Don't expect them to bounce back quickly or in a time frame you think is reasonable. Each one is different. Each one unique. Deep down, they love you, they just may not be able to express that right away. The cycle adults go through in divorce repeats itself for the kids afterward when navigating two households and then again when parents remarry. So, in some ways, they eventually have more experience at this than we do.

We are now at a point where friendship is the main factor between Michael's parents. Now we can't imagine it any other way. You can get there too.

Emotional Growth

Through all the pain I had in dealing with other adults, outside of my parents and stepmom, I have learned how to handle difficult people.

Georgie taught me to try different things and move on to something else if what you were doing was not working. My little brother annoyed me at times, but I loved playing with him. I didn't want to like him or Georgie, but now I do like them. In fact, I love them.

So, get over your differences. Learn to deal with other people. Never regret learning from that.

Even though I was a sheltered, spoiled little brat, I came to terms with everything that happened. I know better now. The divorce didn't have anything to do with us; it had to do with my parents.

Mom and Dad have grown from their experience, we have grown from ours and we have all moved past it. Our situation was a bad one for a long time, but emotional growth has allowed us to be a better family now.

I am excited the most when I see the relationship my family now has through learning to adapt to each other. My mom married my stepdad, John, earlier this year and she invited Dad and Georgie. Yeah, it's weird.

We don't have to go to different houses to see my parents. We celebrate Christmas and other holidays together. I see Mom and John and Dad and Georgie talk to each other. Mom and Georgie hang out together and it's cool.

Even though my parents are not together; they are here for us, they are still our family. I am not saying this will happen with every blended family, but with us, it worked out.

Amazing what kids learn through the difficulties of life. Michael can be around and work with all types of personalities. Some are easier than others, but he can function around pretty much anyone, even when he doesn't want to.

I appreciate the respect that Michael gave me growing up, along with his siblings. I knew it was difficult for them; it was difficult for me at times as well. I wouldn't change any of it, not even the mistakes. We all grew emotionally together and our family is strong.

The "M" in Man

A Man doesn't always get to choose who his family is, but a Man will try to love them anyway. A Man steps up and makes the best of the situation and with those around him. I capitalize the "m" in man because of everything that goes with it: responsibility, maturity, choosing to love, admitting and accepting the fact that you are not always right.

Maturing helped me to become a better person overall, slower to anger, more tolerant. People may still see me frustrated, but generally not angry. Learning patience was a big step for me in becoming a Man.

I trust Michael's Amazing, Fantastic, Terrific, Wonderful story gives you hope. The man he has become was always there; he just had to find him.

<u>Michael's Reflections</u>

- Don't be afraid to contradict others or, more importantly, yourself.

- Get over your differences and learn to deal with people.

- Admit and accept being wrong.

- You can love the people you don't like. Once you learn to love them, then you start to like them, even if at first you didn't want to.

- A Man steps up and makes the best of the situation and with those around him.

Michael's Blender

Activity

Building with Legos

What kid doesn't like to build with Legos? I had them when I was a kid and I still get to "play" with all the "Littles". Life is good!

Recipe

Mom's Mashed Potatoes

Comfort Food at its best!

Building with Legos

Supplies

- ☐ Kids
- ☐ Legos
- ☐ Floor space
- ☐ Imagination

Directions (It's great being a kid again!)

- ☐ Use appropriate Legos for the age group of kids you are "playing" with. So many colors and sizes!

- ☐ Make sure you have plenty of space to build high, long and wide.

- ☐ Use your imagination to create buildings, ships, creatures, etc. Items around you that are not Legos can be added in as well.

- ☐ Have a contest to see who can build the highest tower before it falls.

- ☐ Take pictures and post them, so that you can build over and over without hurt feelings.

Mom's Mashed Potatoes

Ingredients

- ☐ 1 ½ - 2 potatoes per person
- ☐ 1 teaspoon salt
- ☐ ½ - 1 cup milk
- ☐ ½ cup butter

Directions

- ☐ Peel potatoes and cut into 1- inch cubes.
- ☐ Place potatoes in a pan of cold water. (rinse a couple of times before filling the pot).
- ☐ Add salt.
- ☐ Place on medium-high heat and bring to a boil.
- ☐ Reduce heat and cook until the potatoes are easily pierced with a fork.
- ☐ Drain the potatoes, but leave just a small amount of the cooking water.

☐ Add milk. (start on the light side – you can always add more!)

☐ Add butter and combine all ingredients with a mixer until smooth.

Serves 4-6 people

6

I'm Okay.
Are You Okay? –
Jessica's Concern

*"Coming together is a beginning,
staying together is progress,
and working together is success."*
-Henry Ford

"Picture of a Family Bike Ride" by Marisa

JESSICA – Youngest of the "Original 5"

Independent, smart, calm but determined, and logical thinker are all words I would use to describe Jessica. She has taught me to take the time to seek and understand that there are multiple ways of showing you love someone. I have also learned some of the most profound, insightful and sometimes funniest things come from those who are less verbal than I am.

Jessica was dealing with protection from her older siblings and wanted to, in turn, protect them as well. Balancing her role as the youngest and being a peacemaker are paths she focused on.

A nursing student in Georgia, Jessica has a deep love for her family as a daughter, sister and aunt.

Middle Ground

The original youngest, unsure of my role, in a rapidly changing day by day scene. I really didn't know where I stood or if there was a certain role I should claim. In the transition, should I try to have fun so that everyone was okay? Should I be considerate of everyone's feelings? Was I just tagging along? Lots of I don't knows.

Difficult to say what was for sure home, because it changed - a lot. I finally concluded, if there was family where I was, it was "home-ish."

The whirlwind of going house to house and meeting unexpected expectations was like hitting a volleyball to no opponent. The expectations I thought were there, really were not, it was just me. I put pressure on myself to do what I thought other people expected of me.

At each household, I can and did have fun, but not too much fun because I couldn't say one house was more fun than the other. If I did, then it would hurt other peoples' feelings and everyone was in a vulnerable place. I didn't want to step on anyone's toes because of the insecurity everyone was feeling. This was new for everybody.

Jessica was very mature for her age, even at seven years old when I first started dating her father. Jessica's maturity was partially due to having four older siblings as well as her general personality. I can still remember how particular she was, especially about her shoes. So, it was natural for her to be aware of other people's feelings and to make sure she didn't contribute to the hurt they were feeling.

Jessica typically goes with the flow and stays calm. In this, she reminds me of her dad. She has decided, as an adult, to enter the nursing field and will be a soothing person for patients to encounter. I even took her with me when I had to have blood drawn during my pregnancy (I sort of have issues with needles from time to time). Her calming demeanor affects those around her.

Siblings' Pain

Siblings who did have a memory of a loving first marriage were struggling to adapt to the changes of a collaborative family. I was so young that it was not a surprise my parents were divorcing; it made sense. I didn't see any fun between them. So, I adapted quickly to the idea because it was not as big of an issue for me.

I could see it was a big deal for my siblings. They remembered seeing something they didn't think could fail and since I was the youngest, they felt they would have to guard me. I tried to prove to them I wasn't as upset by it, so their stress would be released and they could have fun and not worry about me.

Jessica's perspective is different from her siblings' due to how young she was when the divorce happened. Logic set in for her regarding the relationship between her parents. Much of her life has been lived as a part of two separate households.

The older siblings felt they needed to protect Jessica, but she was more concerned with the pain they were going through and wanted to protect them by showing that she was okay. She just wanted them to have fun and not hurt anymore.

Learning to Love

Learning to love someone who hasn't been there since your birth, is not something you automatically do. You should get to know them in the same way you learn a new friend and how you interact and get to know that person.

The realization of people in your life who add additional love is both a blessing and a lesson. Receiving the warm welcome of love by a different name is the blessing.

My parents both love me, but it is more of a stoic kind of love, more understood. We verbalize it, but not as much or as blatant as my stepmom, Georgie, does. We had to learn a different way to love with a new stepmom who was more verbal, more physical, more direct. There was no misunderstanding of what she felt. I think it was hard for her because we didn't verbalize the way she did, but she knew where we stood.

My stepdad, John, is even more stoic than my parents, so I am more like him and therefore it was easier to understand him. He shows love more through actions, more like I do.

The lesson I have learned was adapting to and understanding there are different ways to interact and show your affection. It doesn't mean love is less or more, just different.

Jessica's perspective on forging new relationships with stepparents, the way you would do the same with a new friend, is insightful. At the core of a great relationship is friendship. Building on this foundation lends itself to the blessing of different types of love from the diverse people you spend time with. Jessica found a way to connect with her stepparents, one easier than the other.

I tend to get excited about pretty much everything. Jessica is more even keel than I am, so we have found a happy medium to balance each other. She is still soaking in everything I say, just not always commenting about it.

Believe me, though, when she does have something to say, it is thought provoking and/or funny. I still remember when she shocked her Uncle Kevin with a joke one time when we were at a family dinner. The expression on his face was priceless. I don't think he believed she had a sense of humor until then.

Busy Life

With multiple siblings, nieces and nephews and busy schedules, life was non-stop. You are always doing something. Going house to house, playing soccer, going to someone's game, watching someone have a baby...busy family, busier because of two households.

Excitement for me was when we celebrated holidays in one location, not separated at noon. I dreaded having to leave at noon on Christmas Day to travel to the other household. The split in time made things awkward and not traditional. We had to get up early, open presents, spend time with the parent(s), etc. So now do we open presents on

Christmas Eve and then go? The other parent(s) also had to spend Christmas alone, which was very depressing for them.

Spending holidays together now, everyone sees the same excitement, spends the same time together and competition is eliminated. We also have fewer goodbyes.

Christmas was split by the noon hour. Not the greatest of circumstances for the kids, but it allowed both parents to spend time with them on Christmas Day. Whirlwind doesn't even begin to cover our experiences of going back and forth between the households and working around schedules. I remember hearing one time how a set of parents decided to have an apartment and a house when dealing with their blended family. The kids would always stay at the house and the parents were the ones who would travel from the house to the apartment. I don't think that would have worked with us, but it is something else to think about in a split family situation.

Ultimately, we decided to simplify things and come together for all holidays and celebrations. To see the kids now, even as adults, more comfortable with the family, is the most rewarding thing to witness. We could never have predicted where we are now, it wasn't even a possibility way back when...

Stepping Stones

My parents and stepparents promoted independence and academic achievement to the point I learned skills to take care of myself in college. I am in a place where I can be more independent than some of my peers. My background has helped to put me where I am in taking care of myself at 20 years old. I want to be successful so that I can give back to my parents what they gave to me growing up. Nursing is a good field to help others because you are always needed and there is no ceiling on what you can learn.

Fostering independence is one of the things that can positively impact kids in a blended family. There are things they deal with their friends do not. Jessica took this lesson to heart and in turn has the desire to not only give back to her family, but her community as well. Always learning, always giving, she is someone we are all proud of and love.

Strengths and Loveable Weaknesses

Lean on each other's strengths. Forgive each other's weaknesses.

Strengths in our family include being good at conflict resolution compared to other families I know, who are split. We have figured things out and how to deal with each other; it's not always smooth, but functional. We laugh a good amount and don't take things too seriously. If we get offended, we get over it quickly and move on for the most part.

Family weaknesses include some insecurity and not being assertive. We sometimes feel a certain way, don't say it right then, it festers, but we eventually work it out. We should just say what we mean right when we feel it instead of beating around the bush. We have quite a bit of stubbornness in our family.

Having the love and support from multiple avenues and in multiple forms has made me sure of who I am and sure of the strengths and loveable weaknesses of my topsy turvy family.

Jessica knows who she is and where she is going. She took the experiences of her diverse family situation and applied it to how she lives her life. Sure, we still have issues at times, what family doesn't? But we love each other, support each other. We know where we lack and where we excel. The great thing about it though, is together we can fill in those gaps and be this all-inclusive family who has fun with each other, makes lasting memories and is full of life!

Jessica's Reflections

- Make sure that everyone knows there is no expectation to feel a certain way about what is going on. You feel how you feel.

- Be open to different people, different interactions and different kinds of love.

- Have fun, not everything is always a happy situation, but know that everyone is okay and be grateful for what you do have.

Jessica's Blender

Activity

Stained Glass Candy Recipe and Activity

This is a favorite recipe and activity we do together on the evening of Thanksgiving. You will need to work fast and the more people, the easier it is. We used to make Stained Glass Candy as a Christmas present for our teachers when we were younger.

Recipe

Cinnamon Swirl Bread (Better Homes and Gardens Biggest Book of Bread Machine Recipes ©2003. Page 51)

Mom makes this bread for me when I am at home. It is one of my favorites.

Stained Glass Candy
(Family Activity)

Supplies

Each batch makes one flavor. We typically double each batch because we have at least 4-6 people helping. We make at least 5-6 flavors to distribute to family and friends.

- ☐ 1 cup white Karo corn syrup
- ☐ 2 cups granulated sugar
- ☐ 2/3 cups water
- ☐ 1-dram (½ teaspoon) oil candy flavoring
- ☐ Food coloring
- ☐ Powdered sugar

Directions

- ☐ Cover two cookie sheets with powdered sugar. Set aside.
- ☐ Cook corn syrup, sugar and water in a heavy saucepan to 300 degrees/hard crack

stage. Use a candy thermometer. Stir occasionally with a wooden spoon. Remove from heat as soon as 300 degrees is reached.

☐ Add oil flavoring and food coloring. Do <u>NOT</u> lean over the pan as oil is added! The fumes are quite strong. Stir well to blend.

☐ Pour liquid candy in thin ribbons onto the powdered sugar covered cookie sheets.

☐ Cut into small pieces as soon as cool enough to handle without sticking to scissors. (Work fast while candy is pliable!) If candy becomes too hard to cut, it may be broken into small pieces, but it will have sharp edges!

☐ Make several batches of different flavors/colors. Place all the candy in a clean pillowcase to mix.

☐ Place in clear glass jars to give as Christmas gifts.

The recipe can be cut in half if working alone, or doubled or tripled if several people are available to help cut.

Candy oils must be used. Oils are available at pharmacy counters in most drug stores or at candy supply stores. They are often found in the cake decorating supplies at hobby stores as well. Look for LorAnn Oils.

Flavor/Color Suggestions:

- ☐ Cinnamon – red
- ☐ Butter Rum – yellow
- ☐ Spearmint – blue
- ☐ Clove - orange
- ☐ Wintergreen – green
- ☐ Root Beer – brown
- ☐ Peppermint – pink
- ☐ Grape – purple
- ☐ Raspberry – blue
- ☐ Watermelon – green
- ☐ Cherry - red

Cinnamon Swirl Bread

Ingredients

- ☐ 1 cup milk
- ☐ 2 eggs
- ☐ 1/4 cup butter
- ☐ 4 cups bread flour
- ☐ 1/4 cup granulated sugar
- ☐ 1 teaspoon salt
- ☐ 1 1/2 teaspoons active dry yeast
- ☐ 1/2 cup chopped pecans
- ☐ 1/2 cup brown sugar
- ☐ 2 teaspoons ground cinnamon
- ☐ 2 tablespoons softened butter
- ☐ Sifted powdered sugar

Directions (made in the bread machine)

- ☐ Add first 7 ingredients to a 2lb. loaf bread machine according to manufacturer's directions.

- ☐ Select dough cycle. When cycle is complete, remove dough. Punch down. Cover and let rest for 10 minutes.

- ☐ For the filling, stir together nuts, brown sugar, and cinnamon. Set aside.

- ☐ Grease two 9x5x3 inch loaf pans. Set aside.

- ☐ Divide dough in half. On a lightly floured surface, roll dough into 14x9 in. rectangle.

- ☐ Spread 1/2 the butter & sprinkle 1/2 the filling.

- ☐ Roll up both short sides into a spiral toward center. Place, rolled side up, in loaf pan. Repeat with other half of dough.

- ☐ Cover and let rise in a warm place about 30 minutes or until nearly double.

- ☐ Bake at 350 degrees for about 30 minutes or until bread sounds hollow when lightly tapped. If necessary, cover with foil the last 10 minutes to prevent over browning.

- ☐ Remove from pan; cool on wire rack.

- ☐ Before serving, sprinkle with powdered sugar.

7

The Power of Going Through

*Jesus looked at them and said,
"With man this is impossible, but
with God all things are possible."
Matthew 19:26 NIV*

"The Family" by Wes

WAYNE – Father of "Original 5"

Minister, leader, teacher, pioneer and my husband are all words I would use to describe Wayne. He has taught me to live life with integrity and to take life more calmly than I have done so in the past. We are opposites in that regard, nothing shakes him too much and I can freak out over the smallest thing, so we balance each other in a good way. Being married to him has helped me to destress, despite the challenges of a blended family situation. And who couldn't use a little more balance in their life?

Wayne was dealing with life as a single dad, then married again all while settling into a new rhythm of life played to a different kind of beat. He and the mother of the "Original 5" resolved to turn around harmful effects on the family and replace the broken strings with ties of unity.

Living in Georgia and married to Georgie, Wayne is the father of six, "uncle" to three and Grandad to seven.

Failure...Not an Option?

Failure wasn't something I expected, certainly not in marriage.

After many years of marriage, then, when things began to break down between Pam and me I figured, "We can fix this." Deeper down I decided that if we can't fix this then I would fix it. And, yes, as you might imagine, that's part of my problem. Self-reliance and personal confidence have their limits and can wear on the nerves of others...especially those closest to you.

In addition to being husband to Pam and father to our five kids, I was also a pastor and I was in corporate sales. Positive things were happening in our community outreach, and I was managing the sales of my employer's products and services over a wide area. In business, I was a troubleshooter, and I sought to be forward-thinking in ministry.

By this point in our marriage a couple of things had begun to weigh on my mind. I saw Pam dealing with more stress and heard her concerns about the challenges of managing our kids and their active schedules. And, because of this and the general toll of ministry/work/family/community/school, etc., and all sorts of other obligations; I saw cracks begin to appear in our relationship, I naturally assumed that all would be worked out, that I would troubleshoot and minister my way to a successful result.

An opportunity came my way, and my career path changed. This allowed me to be closer and more involved at home. This change was a blessing, especially afterward, but in the near term it was almost like it added to the stress between Pam and me. In other words, whatever stress Pam was dealing with seemed to be compounded by my increased presence.

Anyway, despite concerns, I was pretty confident. We had about 18 years of marriage under our belts, a houseful of kids who were doing well, a common faith, money enough to more than pay the bills, and family and friends who encouraged us. Life was mostly good.

The "fixer of things". I can relate to this because I, too, am one who thrives on taking something that is not working and making it what it needs to be. These "projects" are where I focus my creativity in the workplace. The confidence that accompanies a person who is assertive in this area sometime grates on those who deal with issues in a different manner. Resolution does not always come easy when these two forces collide.

Changes in the schedules and routines on the home front can be difficult, especially when there are already tough emotions being expressed. These alterations can put great pressure on a relationship.

Meltdown

Meltdown - - I think I've heard that a thermonuclear meltdown is initiated by a small breakdown or series of breakdowns which cascade into an unstoppable and devastating catastrophe. In April of 2002, I recall that Pam and I discussed our relationship at some length. I was concerned, but I came away from that conversation more or less assured. Love was still there, with some issues, but still love.

Three months later all of that had changed. It was basically over between us. There would be other things to be discussed and efforts to be made. But it was over. It would take another year and a half for our marriage to finish dying.

It would be difficult to describe the tragedy of all of this, especially since we are now very much post-tragedy. At that time and for a long time afterward my heart and mind were in some war zone, and one that I had never anticipated. We were headed toward a breakdown. I began to understand from a personal perspective why God says, "I hate divorce."

The war zone that Wayne describes as going on in his heart and mind was very real. I still remember conversations we had and things I would hear him and the kids express. To see this was heartbreaking. At some point in the beginning of our dating relationship, I wondered if I should back out of the picture and instead encourage some kind of marital reconciliation between these two parents. After much soul searching, however, I realized it was not something that was going to happen between the two of them.

Jayne mentions in her chapter how people outside of a situation sometimes hurt more than help. Wayne also references destructive comments that people felt it was their duty to express about something that had nothing to do with them. Emotions run high at times, but in the end, do these outbursts really help?

Going Through

I sought counsel directly from people who I considered wiser than me. And I listened to advice in the words of just about everyone. Some of it helped; some didn't. Some of it was vile and destructive – even from people who should have known better.

There was, however, counsel that was crucial. Such counsel was crystallized for me with these simple words:

"Whatever you're going through, go on through."

Those were the words that came to me through two separate people at two separate times. I believe they were God's words, given to me by Wayne and Elizabeth. Natural brother and sister, African-American, people I had known for years, without counseling degrees or ministry certifications, they expressed a basic truth that I desperately needed to hear: You are going through something – yes – but go on through.

I clung to those words. I desperately needed what those words represented. They kept me going when other things failed me.

I only wish I could have adequately conveyed their meaning to my family. I feel like I failed them in many ways. But there was always something deeper and stronger in our family than any of our failures.

"...Go on through." Even if all you do is go through the motions, smile and escape at home to comfort from the outside world, it is better than shutting down completely. Bills are still there to be paid, kids to be taken care of, work to be done, food to be prepared, life to be lived. The basics will keep you going and eventually day by day, it will be a little easier to function.

Time Passes, Things Change

Several years passed. The divorce happened. A family was separated. Ministries and careers changed. New marriages began, and the family dynamic became more complex. The whole process was messy at times, and there was much angst as to how to make the new reality a good reality.

I felt bad for our kids. They had to navigate this new world; problem enough for us adults, but for them — wow. It was plain to see that the balancing act for them was always challenging and at times ridiculously so. How could they spend time and energy and affection in ways that would appease parents and extended family, and still grow strong for themselves?

So, for who they were then and especially for who they are now, I am intensely proud of our kids. They have become strong adults, leading their lives, blessing their families and friends. They express an undiminished love for Pam and me, and for our new spouses John and Georgie.

If you haven't already read by now, yes, it's true, our family now shares major family events together. We communicate individually of course but also as a group, as a well-functioning unit. Christmas, Thanksgiving, birthdays, weddings – we engage joyfully and peacefully in the presence of each other. We encourage each other, we joke and kid around, we visit in each other's homes. Pam is kind of like a sister to me, and I count her husband John as a friend. John's kids are part of the crew and they seem to genuinely enjoy being included in this odd family. Georgie and Pam plan family events together. The kids and *grandkids join in and always make things memorable.*

It belabors the point to say this was not always the case, so I trust that our family brings some hope to situations that our readers find themselves in. I'm sure you've figured out that you can't fix everything. I'm sure that if you haven't experienced similar personal tragedy, then you know others who have. Bless them, encourage them, hear their anger, bind their wounds where you can. Pray for them and with them.

I enjoy seeing the interaction between Wayne and Pam now. They function much like our daughter, Jayne, and son, Michael, do. You know, the sister and brother who always picked on each other and still do as adults.

The night before Pam and John married, we were all sitting around our daughter Belinda's table talking after eating a meal together. Pam's sister Roni and her husband

Rick were there as well. Wayne said something smart aleck to Pam and she threw something at him from across this very long table. She has good aim! We laughed and Rick and Roni had a somewhat interesting look on their faces. The last time they had been around all of us was at the beginning of our reconciliation and when we weren't on speaking terms much at all!

Belinda brings up an interesting point in her chapter. She is thankful for having stepparents who are secure in their relationships. Stepparents who understand the time bio parents need with their kids. Stepparents who get it that bio parents can still be friends and even have fun around each other. Stepparents that are not afraid of peace. I have the best stepparent partner in John. The "Original 5" have been through a lot and to see them have a stepdad like him makes me happy.

Thoughts...and small steps

I leave you with a few thoughts:

Keep the commitments you still have. After a few years apart from Pam, I took a job a couple of hours away. It was a big step to make a move farther from our kids, since most of them were still with Pam. Georgie made the determination right along with me to stay constantly involved in the kids' lives. Long hours and long miles of driving were invested in getting to games and graduations and dozens of everyday events that were important to our kids. Pam also increasingly helped in keeping them involved with Georgie and me.

People in the middle aren't pawns in a game. Again, it's so obvious but so hard to avoid in the heat of human emotions: The war you think you're having with someone else is never an excuse to make a casualty out of others. Kids still want to be kids, friends still want to be friends, in-laws may still want to be connected. Get over it and make it a little easier for others to still relate to the ones you may now be separated from.

Small steps of good will are necessary (of course!). And from the foundation of the small, be ready to take leaps of trust when the time is right.

A couple of years after we moved away, Pam also found a need to move, and it was closer in our direction. It became obvious that she could use some assistance in getting situated. I already knew what we'd probably end up doing. Georgie approached me, stating the obvious.

"You know, Pam's moving."

"Yeah, I know."

"You know, she's moving to such and such place, around such and such time."

"Yeah – I know."

"I think she needs some help."

"Yeah...I know."

"I think we need to help her."

"Yeah...I KNOW!"

We ended up helping Pam unload her U-Haul on a hot summer day in Rome, GA. I was up in the back of the van sweating. I was the only one in the van sweating. (Ok, to be fair, Georgie and Pam were on the ground and in the storage unit, also sweating).

Oddly, while unloading, I ended up in the position of being supervised by both Pam and

Georgie. Grinning a little too much, Georgie asked me, "So Wayne, what does it feel like – taking orders from your wife and your ex-wife?" I remember responding, "Seems like a vision of hell to me!"

That event was substantial for all of us. All of us working together, trusting each other, talking like people do when faced with a shared task.

That environment has developed into what you're now reading about: A family- A little odd, once broken, now healthy and growing and wanting to be something better. I hope we bring you a little more, well, hope. We're all where we are, and we can't change what brought us here. We can, however, change in small and large ways where we're going.

I was nervous. Here we all were (Wayne, Pam, Wes and I), together, moving Pam's things into a storage unit and Wes, who was in pre-school at the time, was trying to tell everyone what to do, even Pam. Yikes! Were we going to get through this intact and come together again peacefully? So, being who I am and pushing a little all the time, I decided to break the edginess with a little humor and ask the question Wayne describes above. It worked! Success!

Each encounter after this first one added another layer of ease we continued to build on. I still remember Wayne and John meeting for the first time. They both have a love of wood and wood projects. Wayne is more into large outdoor projects and John, smaller more detailed projects. (Pam and I utilize their talents when planning family Christmas gifts!) Wayne and John hit it off right away with their shared connection.

We are close. We connect and we share a love of this family. What more could you ask for?

Wayne's Reflections

- Keep the commitments you still have.

- People in the middle aren't pawns in a game.

- Small steps of good will are necessary.

Wayne's Blender

Activity

Bonfire with hot dog roast, marshmallows and s'mores

We often host a bonfire at our home whenever family comes over. Most times the creek is running close by and the kids play after eating. With the size of our family, this is an economical way to feed them all while still having fun!

Recipe

Moody's Impact1! Chili

Impact1! is the social entrepreneurship we created in 2014 for men in Chattanooga, TN, who are motivated to move forward regardless of their background. We engage these men in seven weeks of Life Success Strategies and Construction Skills Training. The men graduate and then have the opportunity to work on paid construction projects utilized as transitional employment.

I have made this chili several times for the men of Impact1! and they all have the recipe. It is definitely a "Man's" version of chili with it's simple ingredients.

Bonfire with Hot Dog Roast, Marshmallows & S'mores

Supplies

- ☐ Bonfire
- ☐ Thin tree branches
- ☐ Hot dogs
- ☐ Hot dog buns
- ☐ Condiments
- ☐ Chips
- ☐ Drinks
- ☐ Marshmallows
- ☐ Graham crackers
- ☐ Chocolate bars

Directions

- ☐ Start bonfire.
- ☐ Cut roasting sticks from branches.
- ☐ Place hot dogs on roasting sticks and cook for desired doneness.

- ☐ Serve with buns, condiments, chips and drinks.

- ☐ Place marshmallows on roasting sticks and cook for desired doneness.

- ☐ Eat marshmallows plain or place on graham cracker covered in chocolate and place an additional graham cracker on top for a S'more.

- ☐ Enjoy family time!

Moody's Impact1! Chili

Ingredients

- ☐ 2 pounds of ground meat
- ☐ Olive oil
- ☐ Garlic powder
- ☐ One 24oz. jar of spaghetti sauce (roasted garlic type seems to work well)
- ☐ One 14 oz. jar of medium salsa
- ☐ Two 16 oz. cans of black beans
- ☐ Two 16 oz. cans of dark red kidney beans
- ☐ Chili powder
- ☐ Black pepper
- ☐ Salt
- ☐ Dash of steak sauce and/or barbecue sauce

Directions

☐ Sauté meat in olive oil with a dash of garlic powder.

☐ Add spaghetti sauce, salsa and beans.

☐ Season to taste with remaining ingredients.

8

Adventures, Positivity & Predestination

""Life is nothing but a series of opportunities to move toward, move through and move on."
– Amy Dickinson

"Bain Family" by Robby

PAM - Mother of "Original 5"

Virtual assistant, crafting genius, planner, sarcastic/hilarious humor and my friend are all words I would use to describe Pam. She has taught me to look at life from a different perspective and realize that introverts are some of the coolest people you can know.

Pam was dealing with life after the divorce as a single mom, married, then single again all while navigating a sense of balance with highs, lows and in-betweens. She and the father of the "Original 5" decided to break the negative roller coaster we had all been riding and replace it with the hope that we could exist together in peace.

Living in Georgia and married to John, Pam is the mother of five, stepmother of three, "aunt" to one and Nana to seven.

Life Scrambled

I've always heard life is what happens while you're busy making plans*. Sometimes life gets scrambled like fluffy Lambchop eggs

(scrambled eggs were called Lambchop eggs to
get the kids to eat them!).

*Allen Saunders – 1957 January, Reader's
Digest, Quotable Quotes, Page 32, The
Reader's Digest Association. (Verified on
paper)*

I am the biological mother to five of the most
amazing people you'd ever be blessed to meet.
Okay, I may be a little biased, but I really loved
raising my kids and watching them turn into
productive members of society. Each one is a
unique individual. Each one came with her/his
own set of challenges. And then their parents
made everything so much more complicated by
getting a divorce.

Now these wonderful children had to deal
with being young teens and pre-teens with
parents who couldn't get along. We were so busy
blaming each other that we failed to see how we
were affecting our children. Along the way, they
gained two stepparents – one wanted to
reconcile the family; one wanted to keep the

family torn up. For eight years, we lived in this turmoil. We forgot that we said, "Til death do us part."

"Til death do us part." I love Pam's take on this familiar vow. Divorce doesn't end a relationship between two people who share kids together. Regardless of what that relationship is; good, bad or ugly, they are connected because of the kids. They will always be connected, so why not go ahead and choose restoration?

Overwhelming Emotions & Connection via Conversation

During these eight long years, there were so many emotions to work through — both mine and the kids. I was a scared, often lonely, jealous, overwhelmed mom. When the kids were away, I imagined all sorts of scenarios where the kids loved their dad more than they loved me; where I would end up alone, homeless, and without my kids; where my kids would grow up and be broken people.

All was not so glum. There were moments of "Peace" when all was right in my world. At any given time, I would receive a warm hug from one of the kids. My son and I had wrestling matches on the living room floor where we would say, in our best Southern accents, "I do declare, this carpet needs a good cleaning!" The girls and I spent hours surfing the web and having "Sex Education 101". We had long talks about "Everything". We spent hours/days at soccer games. We attended FFA events. And all of it was covered with lots of laughter.

Depression and pessimism have always been things I've struggled against. There came a point when I finally realized that I truly am the only one who can control how I react to life. I decided that I wasn't going to live a "Garbage In-Garbage Out" life anymore. I was tired of being overwhelmed. I was tired of being broken.

Pam made a choice, we made a choice, the kids made a choice. The operative word here is "choice". Focusing on the "garbage" as Pam refers to, not only delays peace in your family, but the emotional turmoil of all this negativity controls you. Nobody wants to be controlled. Yes, there are still positive moments and laughter and peacefulness in the separate households, but there is still the brokenness of a family not functioning as a whole.

We all have our own individual issues. Pam is going to show you how she worked on hers instead of continuing to let her imagination make her believe the worst. Today she is loved, surrounded by us all and the cracks in our shell are filled with the mortar of healthy memories.

Personal Development

I started reading everything I could find online about choosing to live "Positively". I found positive quotes, wrote them out, and taped them to the refrigerator and the bathroom mirror. I searched the Bible for

God's promises and repeated them to myself regularly. I listened to TED talks. I started a new hobby to help focus my mind. I threw myself into my work and did all I could to excel. I prayed and cried out to God. In November of 2008, I sought God and asked Him what to do. I received one word deep in my soul, "Wait". So, I waited not knowing for what or how long.

Personal development is something we all can benefit from on a continual basis. A plant still needs sunshine and water and sometimes a little food to be what it is designed to be. When the plant is harvested, that which is left adds minerals back to the soil for the next cycle. What are you designed for? What can you do in the personal development arena to add to your life?

Pam was searching for answers and even though she did not receive them right away, she didn't give up.

Hope

A year and a half later, I became a single parent again. The moment I announced to my kids' father that I was getting a divorce, he and his wife asked, "How can we help?" The turning point we had all been longing for had finally arrived. They actually helped me unload my moving truck!

I experienced independence on a whole new level. I moved away from everyone that I knew, bought and set up a home for myself and two youngest children. Together we maintained our home and made improvements to the house. The kids went to school. I worked from home. Every other weekend, they traveled 65 miles to spend with their father. But now there was no fear of loss or competition.

You have already read Wayne's tale of this first collaboration and it had its funny moments. We were all taking that first step which was a little scary and exciting and overwhelming. What the future held at that point, we didn't know. Pam embraced her new life in a new place. Michael and Jessica jumped into this journey with her and were the first ones to be a part of the steps we continued to take.

I still remember one of our first dinners together in a public place (at a Mexican restaurant, of course – we all enjoy Mexican food!). Pam and Wayne both had to use reading glasses at this point in their life. I still haven't had to use these dreaded things yet, so I was teasing them both. Pam couldn't find hers, so Wayne offered his to her so she could read her bill before paying. I watched them and was amazed at the glimpse of something so simple appearing normal and comfortable between them. It would prove to be the first of many small steps. Don't be afraid to reach out in small ways, even if they fail at first. Who knows, you may start the rebuilding of your blended family with just a pair of reading glasses.

The Challenge of Removing Self

I started dating a wonderful man with three kids – one grown and two younger kids at home. When our kids met, they all accepted each other. We all bonded quickly. His younger kids and my grandkids are all in the same age range. Together, with my kids' half brother, they became the "Littles".

We were all invited to the grandkids birthday parties (February, March, April, May, June). So, somewhat begrudgingly, we attended these events. And we, the parents, avoided each other.

And then our oldest said she would host Thanksgiving, and she expected us all to be there – and be nice! We attended, and we, the parents, were cordial.

And then the kids decided they didn't want to have to do multiple Christmases with their siblings just so their parents wouldn't have to be there together. We decided one parent would host and all would attend. And then slowly, so slowly, we started to join in the same conversations with our children, their spouses, our grandkids.

Picture us, as if we are part of a flip book (remember those?). With each "page" (event), we inch closer to each other and eventually start talking and sharing and laughing together. The flip took time, but each get together moved us a step closer.

We celebrated Christmas one year at Pam's house and Wayne was in her bathroom downstairs. We heard a crash and then Wayne came out. The bi-fold doors in her bathroom had fallen and Wayne was putting them back up. The moment was a little awkward, so Pam asked if the doors had hit him on the head. He said no, to which she replied, "Darn, my trap didn't work!" We all looked at each other and fell into a fit of laughter.

John started dating Pam when we were at the beginning of our new journey together. So, he has been there right along with us and seen our craziness and has bonded with everyone.

We can honestly say John and Pam have become our friends and our family.

Peace Through the Journey

At some point, I decided that I needed to forgive my kids' dad for everything (real and imagined) if we were to ever get over our past. Not just say I forgive him, but actually "Forgive". I wrote multiple letters and destroyed them. I finally sent one, and he responded in kind. The Bible says that God forgives and forgets our sins once we have repented. I never understood that, but I have forgotten so many of the details now. When you stop rehearsing them in your head, they tend to fade away. Praise God!

And then we had graduations - one college and one high school in the same year. Now we even had our parents in attendance! It was slightly awkward, but we all survived.

A few years later, we had another set of graduations – one master's degree and one high school. And by some miracle, we found

*ourselves laughing and enjoying each other's
company. We took pictures of all of us
together as one big family.*

If I had one moment to pick that was the best in the restoration of our family, it would be the one where Pam and Wayne forgave each other. I was privileged to witness their responses to each other. My heart still swells at the thought of where they have come from to where they are now. Friends.

Our extended families haven't had the opportunity to be around us as much as we are around each other, obviously (they all live in other states). But when they are around they see us as we are now, different from before. One together family.

Last Christmas, John and Pam gave us a present, one that was memorable and fun! We all took pictures together with a hired photographer. Now with 23 of us in this bunch, it is hard to get us all together at the same time. We were missing our daughter, Jayne and her family and John's oldest son, Corey as well. One of these days, we will be able to have the whole crew together at one event and the picture will tell it all.

Where Are We Now?

Somehow, I became friends with my kids' stepmom. We have learned that we have very different strengths. We have learned that we balance each other quite well. Where I'm an introvert and can set up a pretty good plan, she's an extrovert that can execute those plans. We swapped hosting the Christmas gatherings each year. We spent time together planning a wedding. We made gifts for the kids and grandkids. We collaborated on all the family gatherings. We leaned on each other when there were heavy things going on in life.

A few years later, and I am now newly and happily married. Everyone that could be there was at our wedding. We shared the day with seven of our eight kids! Our friends, the Moody Family, were there. At first, I felt really strange about inviting them, but as one of our kids said, "At this point, it would be strange if you didn't invite them. We share all of our special family events together." It was a beautiful event filled with love and laughter.

My husband's oldest son fits right in the same age as my kids. Since he lives so far away, they finally got to meet at our wedding. His younger kids fit right in with their new nieces and nephews. My kids' brother calls us Aunt Pam and Uncle John. He calls our younger kids his cousins. All seven of the grandkids call my husband "Pop".

It wasn't easy, and it wasn't quick. There are still challenges to be faced. There are still old feelings of hurt and anger that try to rear their ugly heads. When they do, I must look them in the eye and firmly tell them they are not welcome. They've been banished.

The blessings we have received through working together for the good of our family are immeasurable. Our children still have parents that love them. Our grandchildren have grandparents that love them. There is no animosity. There is no bickering. There is no *competition. We are all here together for the good of this family **'til death do us part.***

Sometimes life gets better when it ends up as a scrambled crazy mixed-up family.

I never thought Pam and I would end up friends, especially with how different we are from each other. But, "Wow!", we complement each other in ways that make our relationship special. We share this family together and now she is also a stepmom just like me!

Again, this journey was not always what it is now and we have all had our share of ups and downs. The invitation to Pam and John's wedding was wonderful and we enjoyed celebrating another family milestone together. We met John's family and his oldest son for the first time and look forward to more as time allows.

Pam brings up another thing to consider and that is when the past threatens what you have worked so hard to put together. Again, choices must be made. Do you go backwards or do you keep moving forward? We know the answer in our family!

Pam's Reflections

This journey has been challenging and rewarding. I had a lot of personal growth to work through. Some of the quotes that were instrumental to my growth are included here.

- "Nothing is impossible, the word itself says 'I'm possible'!" ~Audrey Hepburn

- The Four Agreements ~Don Miguel Ruiz
   1. Be impeccable in your speech.
   2. Don't take anything personally.
   3. Never assume.
   4. Always do your best.

- "If you don't have time to do it right, when will you have time to do it over?" ~John Wooden

- "Finally, with courage in your heart and with God by your side you take a stand, you take a deep breath and you begin to design the life you want to live as best as you can." The Awakening ~Virginia Marie Swift

Pam's Blender

Activity

The Grinchiest Piñata

This was a part of our Christmas celebration last year. All the "Littles" had their turn at the "Grinch".

Recipe

Flax Cookies

Flax Cookies are a family favorite and requested often.

The Grinchiest Piñata

Supplies for making The Grinchiest Piñata

- ☐ Thin cardboard (like cereal boxes)
- ☐ Packing tape or colored duct tape
- ☐ Tissue paper – red for the hat
- ☐ Tissue paper – dark green for eyebrows, nose, mouth
- ☐ Tissue paper – light green for the face
- ☐ Yellow construction paper for the eyes
- ☐ Red marker for the eyes
- ☐ Cotton balls for the hat trim
- ☐ Glue
- ☐ Strong string/rope for hanging
- ☐ Candy and small toys for filling

Directions

- ☐ Draw and cut out the shape x 2.

- ☐ Draw the Grinch face on the front.

- ☐ Cut enough 2-inch-wide strips of the same cardboard to go all the way around your piñata.

- ☐ Use the tape to attach the 2" wide strips to the back. Creativity will make it fit.

- ☐ Poke a couple of holes and add the string/rope hanger. Add extra tape.

- ☐ Lay the front piece on top of the completed edge and tape it to the 2" wide strips.

- ☐ Cut a small flap in the back for filling.

- ☐ Cut yellow construction paper eyes. Glue onto face. Use the red marker to add details.

- ☐ Cut tissue paper into 1" squares. You'll need a lot of this!

- ☐ Using the eraser end of a pencil, wrap the tissue around the pencil, dip in glue, and stick it to the cardboard cutout.

- ☐ Fill in each section according to the picture.

- ☐ Glue cotton balls to the trim section of the hat and pompom.

- ☐ Fill the piñata, tape the opening closed then cover the back with tissue paper.

Flax Cookies

Ingredients

- ☐ 1 cup butter
- ☐ 1 cup brown sugar
- ☐ 1 cup granulated sugar
- ☐ 2 eggs
- ☐ 1 teaspoon vanilla
- ☐ 1 teaspoon baking soda
- ☐ 1 teaspoon baking powder
- ☐ ½ teaspoon salt
- ☐ ½ cup ground flax
- ☐ 2 cups all-purpose flour
- ☐ 1 cup oatmeal
- ☐ 1 cup pecans or almonds—chopped
- ☐ 2 cups chocolate chips
- ☐ ½ cup dates

Directions

- ☐ Cream butter and sugars together.
- ☐ Add eggs and vanilla.
- ☐ Add dry ingredients.
- ☐ Add last 3 ingredients.
- ☐ Bake at 350 degrees for 10 minutes

Try various substitutions and combinations such as pecans, coconut, cranberries, butterscotch chips, etc.

This recipe came from Dr. Larry Dahlen at Mount Marty College, School of Anesthesia. He's not sure where it came from originally.

9

Balancing the Crew

"We aren't STEP,
We aren't HALF,
We're just FAMILY."
– Unknown

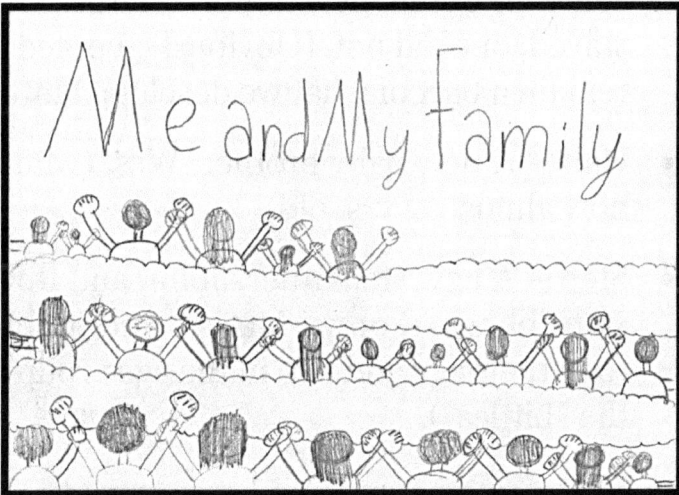

"Me and My Family" by Alaina

BALANCING THE CREW - Additions to the "Original 5"

Step, Half, Step

A new dance move? Not quite. The "Original 5" picked up a few people along their path to complete the blended family they have now.

- Step – Two stepparents were the first to come into the new family status. One stayed, one did not. (Obviously, I opted to remain a part of what we developed into).

- Half – A new baby brother, Wes. (who is now almost 12 yrs. old).

- Step – A new stepfather, John, and three stepsiblings, Corey, Marisa and Robby (one their age and two in the age group of the "Littles").

Outlaws

Outlaws...all joking aside, we are so happy to have wonderful people who are married to three of the "Original 5". The interesting thing about these three is they too, come from blended families.

- Alan – Belinda's other half

- Christopher Alan – husband of Jayne

- Brooke – wife of Michael

Blended Kids of All Ages (the "Littles") and Corey

The term, the "Littles" came about for the sake of simplicity. The "Original 5" have nieces and nephews, a half brother and two stepsiblings all in the same age group.

- Wes – son of Wayne and Georgie.

- Venessa, Alaina, Daniel and Brenden – kids of Belinda and Alan.

- Cassidy and Chloe – children of Jayne and Christopher Alan.

- Audrey – daughter of Michael and Brooke.

- Marisa and Robby – daughter and son of John (Pam is their stepmom).

These ten kids, ages nine months to fourteen years old, function more like cousins (which some of them are).

- Then we have Corey – son of John (Pam is his stepmom).

I list Corey separately because he is in the age group of the "Original 5" and not considered one of the "Littles".

23 and Counting

With two of the "Original 5" unmarried and the addition of their adult stepsibling Corey, not to mention the "Littles". We have no idea how many this family will grow to. We are not even sure if our three kids who are married are done having kids. Check back with us in about 10 years. I am sure we will have more stories to share.

Commitments

When you marry someone, you take on everything about that person – their kids, their vocation, their values, even their former spouse. This is not something to be taken lightly. Sacrifices will need to be made, priorities will need to be changed. If this is not something you are willing to do, please rethink jumping into a blended family. It's not for everyone.

Those of you that have chosen to love your new family, and are determined it will be a rewarding experience, I commend you! One of my pet peeves is a stepparent who doesn't care about their stepkids. Why did you marry into a blended family if it was not what you really wanted in the first place??!! Sometimes you will need to pick the kids up from soccer practice, communicate with the other household regarding schedules and maybe even write out a child support check. You chose this - live up to your responsibilities!

Blended not Broken

Blended not Broken. I have seen this term used multiple times in blended family materials. The term not only is a play on a secret agent's favorite drink, but it also visualizes something that was once broken and is now repaired. Not made new, but repaired.

Think of adding a new connection to the cable line in your home. What do you do? Completely replace it with a new cable? No, you splice it to add the new connection. It is not the same as before, but it still works and the connection you desire is still there.

What's Next?

As I was writing this book, I realized it was impossible to convey all I wanted to in one publication. We have so much more to share – stories from the spouses of the "Original 5", backgrounds of John and I, Corey's perspective and of course, the "Littles" have their own version of our craziness.

We would like for you, the reader, to see more of what we are and in turn, realize you are not alone. We have set up a Facebook page where we will share stories and "Blenders" and there is already talk about a sequel to this book. Please search "Navigating a Blended Family" to like and follow the "Original 5". We look forward to seeing you!

Georgie's Reflections

- Family additions and their diverse backgrounds contribute to the lessons and memories of a blended family.

- Blended family commitments are to be taken seriously. Know what you are getting yourself into because it will affect everyone if you don't.

- Blending is like splicing, the desired connections are still made but through repair, not replacement.

Georgie's Blender

Activity

Family Event Planning

Pam and I have so much fun planning family events. Here is where our creativity shines! We plan throughout the year for Christmas by utilizing Pinterest. Then at Thanksgiving, we make a final list and divide and conquer! Please visit www.pinterest.com and check it out!

Recipe

Enchiladas

Michael likes my enchiladas. His exact quote was, "Anything with beef and cheese is considered comfort food." You can imagine, I made this quite a bit as the kids were growing up!

This is also a family activity type of recipe. One person is not capable of doing all the steps by themselves without major time involvement. Making this a fun family time just adds to all the yumminess!

Family Event Planning

Supplies

- ☐ Pinterest
- ☐ Creativity
- ☐ Supplies from your final list

Directions

- ☐ Start a "secret" Pinterest page and share it with the parent(s) in the other household.
- ☐ Pin anything that sparks your creativity, for the event you are planning, over a pre-designated period.
- ☐ Decide on which activities you will engage in at your next family event.
- ☐ Make a list and divide up the responsibilities.
- ☐ Family Fun Event!

Georgie's Enchiladas

Ingredients

- ☐ 2 ½ pounds ground meat
- ☐ 1 large container of sour cream
- ☐ 1 regular sized bag of shredded cheddar cheese
- ☐ 2 packages of flour tortillas
- ☐ 2-3 cans of refried beans
- ☐ 1 regular sized bag of shredded Mexican blend cheese
- ☐ 1 large jar of salsa
- ☐ Vegetable oil of choice
- ☐ Garlic powder
- ☐ Salt
- ☐ Pepper
- ☐ Cilantro
- ☐ Jalapeños (optional)

Directions

- ☐ Pre-heat oven to 350 degrees.

- ☐ Heat vegetable oil in skillet.

- ☐ Add garlic powder.

- ☐ Brown meat in skillet.

- ☐ Season to taste with salt and pepper.

- ☐ Place browned meat in large bowl and add entire container of sour cream and entire bag of shredded cheddar cheese.

- ☐ Heat vegetable oil in a different skillet.

- ☐ Fry tortillas for 10-15 seconds until tortilla bubbles up. Place tortilla on plate.

- ☐ Spoon refried beans on fried tortilla.

- ☐ Add beef mixture on top of refried beans.

- ☐ Roll tortillas and place in baking dish.

- ☐ Add salsa, a regular bag of Mexican blend shredded cheese and cilantro to top of assembled tortillas. Garnish with jalapeños if desired. Spread all toppings evenly.

- ☐ Bake tortillas for 20 minutes at 350 degrees until cheese is melted.

Notes

In Closing

You don't have to have all the answers, we certainly don't. Reach out to each other and keep trying even if it doesn't go so well the first time around. Little by little, your small start will grow into the blended family you are destined to become. What will your blended family look like?

Free Download

What do you do when your family blend isn't as smooth as you would like for it to be?

Download "When the Blender Breaks"

www.facebook.com/navigatingablended family

www.ingramcontent.com/pod-product-compliance
Lightning Source LLC
Chambersburg PA
CBHW051958090426
42741CB00008B/1448